John Lennon:
The Boy Who Became a Legend

By

Michael A. Hill

John Lennon:

Penin Inc Publishing, LLC

Copyright © 2013 Michael A. Hill

All rights reserved. Published in the United States of America

John Lennon-The Boy Who Became A Legend / Michael A. Hill – 1st U.S. edition

Library of Congress cataloging in publication data

ISBN 978-1542611770

www.OnTheRockBooks.com

Contact details

michael.hill@bigpond.com

Phone 61 417 312 245

6/35 Jells Road   Wheelers Hill 3150   Australia

Contents

	Foreword	6
	Introduction	8
1	*Beyond Imagining*	12
2	*War Infants*	18
3	*Traumatic Times*	29
4	*From Mummy to Mimi*	40
5	*Infants*	49
6	*Neighbourhood Life*	65
7	*Junior School*	77
8	*Entertainment*	87
9	*Mucking Around*	95
10	*Lennon and Tarbuck*	107
11	*Last Days at Dovedale*	113
12	*Grammar School*	121
13	*Punishment*	133

14	*Classroom Clown*	138
15	*Art and Writing*	146
16	*Running Wild in Wales*	153
17	*Being a Nuisance*	158
18	*Money*	164
19	*Growing Up*	173
20	*Scousers*	182
21	*Amsterdam*	186
22	*Musical Destiny*	192
23	*The Quarry Men*	199
24	*Going Nowhere*	206
25	*Quarry Bank Remembered*	213
26	*Musical Families*	219
27	*Musical Foundations*	225
28	*Merseybeat*	232
29	*Anguish*	243
30	*Little Richard*	249
31	*Divergence*	264

32	*Taking Off*	270
33	*A Fascinating Photo*	278
34	*Reconnecting*	288
	Author's Acknowledgements	304
	Bibliography	306

John Lennon:

Foreword

At Quarry Bank School in Liverpool, I remember Michael Hill as being taller than the rest of us, with a shock of red hair. We both started our first year in 1952, resplendent in our new uniforms, including white-striped caps that identified us as Newts, the name for first-year boys. The two of us studied, as all first-year boys did, in Bailey House on the first floor of the two-storey red-brick building which still forms part of what is now Calderstones School.

Rod Davis at Quarry Bank, May 1957.

Neither of us suspected that another young Newt– a certain John Lennon–would eventually change the world. We had both known him from an early age, Michael as a fellow pupil of John's at Dovedale Road Primary School near Penny Lane, and myself as a classmate in the Sunday School at St. Peter's Church in Woolton. Both of these places would play their part in the history of The Beatles in later years.

My memories are of climbing over the school wall at lunchtimes and going out of bounds for a stroll down to Penny Lane, taking care to avoid the headmaster's house, which stood behind the fire station. I recall eating chips in the bus shelter on the roundabout, getting our hair cut at Bioletti's and trying to write down the words of songs as we listened to records in the branch of NEMS on Allerton Road. These were the innocent pleasures of our schoolboy years. As he relates in this book, Michael's own lunchtime activities were to exert a significant influence on the direction of John's future career.

Michael's recollections have that authentic flavour which, unlike most Beatle-related writing, comes from a person who was actually there during John's younger years and who lived through them alongside him.

Thanks Michael– you brought it all back to me.

Rod Davis

Introduction

From when we were infants in our first year at school and as we grew up together, my friend John Lennon had kept me amused and diverted in the classroom and playground with his witty and clever use of English, his drawings and his hilarious and often outrageous antics.

In our teenage years, as I in my turn entertained him at my family home by playing records from my growing collection of top twenty hits, country music and jazz, little did I realise that I was profoundly influencing the future direction of his life. I didn't foresee the impact my records, and one record in particular, would have on him. By his own admission, hearing this record for the first time proved to be a turning point of his life. It awoke in him a latent musical and creative talent that led to his forming the most successful pop music group ever, The Beatles, and a highly creative song writing partnership–two ventures that would fundamentally influence the course of popular music throughout the world.

How this came to pass and the events that shaped the character of the young John Lennon is a fascinating story that began during the Second World War in August 1940 in the port city of Liverpool in the northwest of England. The city at the time was under siege by Hitler's air force.

The Boy Who Became a Legend

In between night-time bombing raids, two baby boys were born, only ten days and a couple of miles apart. Those two boys, born so close to each other in both time and space, under the same star sign of Libra, were destined to grow up together, to attend the same schools and to become good friends.

The first born, Mike Hill (as I was known at school), would grow up to become a well-known figure in the international business of marine insurance. The second born, John Lennon, who I knew so well through the long years of schooling we shared, was lazy and lethargic. Apart from playing a mouth organ occasionally, he had no interest or ability in music before he was fifteen years old, yet he would become world famous, beyond his or anyone else's imagination, as a rock music star, songwriter and peace activist. Not bad for someone who, after twelve years of education, left school without a single qualification, and was regarded by his school - and by many of his peers - as one of the boys least likely to succeed. How wrong can you be!

Numerous books have been written about John Lennon since his meteoric rise to world prominence as the founder and leader of The Beatles, mostly after his senseless murder in New York City in 1980. Regrettably, much of what is written about him in these books, as well as much of the information on the Internet, is wrong or incomplete. This is especially so as regards his early life and the crucial events that led him to become a musician. Yet books continue to be published, and films to be produced, that perpetuate the myths of the John Lennon story.

Of course, there were quite a few people who went to school with John Lennon, but I am one of only a very few who did so for almost the entire period of his schooling. We were in the same academic year throughout and in the same class most of the time. Always we were in the same group of friends.

Thanks to our long and intimate friendship, I was able to observe John Lennon closely throughout his formative years, from the age of five when we met, to seventeen when we began to go our separate ways. Since then, I have had a lifetime to reflect on how his childhood experiences, some of them traumatic, profoundly shaped his adult attitudes and character. The ancient Chinese proverb, 'In the boy the man', seems particularly apt in the case of John Lennon. By writing this book I hope to set the record straight and to provide unique and revealing insights into the boy I knew who grew up to become the man the world knew.

If I were able to ask him, perhaps John Lennon wouldn't feel that our schooldays were the happiest days of our lives. Still, we did have a lot of laughs and a lot of fun along the way - from the innocence of our pre-pubescent boyhood to the stresses of developing manhood, and from life as infants in war-torn Liverpool to the thrill of experiencing together in our mid-teens the new cultural phenomenon of American rock 'n' roll.

And I hope, as you read this book, you too find some fun and some interest in my recollections and observations on the

The Boy Who Became a Legend

making of John Lennon, the boy who became a legend.

Chapter 1

Beyond Imagining

At Quarry Bank High School in Liverpool, as the bell rang to signal the lunch break at the end of morning lessons, the teacher promptly closed the book he had been using with form 4c and, with a cursory nod of his head in the direction of the classroom door, dismissed the class. Four boys who had been sitting together at the back of the room were among the first out of the door, heading directly to the bicycle sheds. Quickly locating their bikes among the hundreds in the racks, they unlocked them, leapt into the saddle and pedaled furiously out through the main school gates and down Harthill Road. It was a cool sunny day in April 1956 - the first day back at school after the two weeks holiday for Easter.

These four boys flying down the hill were John Lennon, aged fifteen; his friend and inseparable companion, Pete Shotton aged fourteen, my best friend Don Beattie, and me, both aged fifteen. While we had all been friends for years, John and I had known each other longer than we had known the other two: we had attended primary school together from the age of five before going on to the same grammar school when we were eleven.

The Boy Who Became a Legend

According to the school rules, we were supposed to remain at school during the lunch break and eat the hot meal provided in the canteen, for which our families gave us the weekly payment–five shillings or so–every Monday morning. But instead of being well-behaved students who obeyed school rules, the four of us had got into the habit of leaving school at lunchtimes and cycling down to my house about a mile away. My mother had returned to full-time work - she was the manageress of a ladies' fashion shop in downtown Liverpool - when I was ten or eleven years old, so my house was free of parents on weekdays for the whole time I was at grammar school. This, and the fact that we lived not far from the school, and not much further from John's house, made it a convenient place for us to meet at lunchtime during term and at any time during school holidays. During our fourth and fifth years at Quarry Bank, 1955-1957, it became a regular routine, and we spent lunchtimes together at my house on most school days.

My family house was a two-storey semi-detached in Dovedale Road in the suburb of Mossley Hill, about five miles south of the city centre of Liverpool. To get there from school, we rode between the sandstone walls of Harthill Road and into Allerton Road, passing the fire station referred to in Lennon and McCartney's "Penny Lane", continued down Rose Lane, and then turned right into Dovedale Road. My house, number 69, was on the right-hand side of the road. It took us less than ten minutes to cycle there from school.

John Lennon:

Usually, having freewheeled down Rose Lane to the junction with Dovedale Road, I would turn right to my house while the other three cycled on to the fish and chip shop that stood on the right-hand side of Rose Lane on the hill leading up to the railway station. There they bought fish and chips–and often some of the potato scallops that John in particular was inordinately fond of–and brought them back to the house, well wrapped up in greaseproof paper and several layers of newspaper. Meanwhile, I would be busy getting things ready, warming the plates in the oven, buttering a few slices of bread and making us each a mug of hot Cadbury's Bournville Cocoa from the packet I kept hidden behind some books in the bookcase in my bedroom. The reason I hid it was that I didn't want my mother to know that I was entertaining John Lennon and other friends, while eating greasy takeaway food at the house, when by rights I should have been at school eating the healthier school dinners for which she had shelled out from her hard-earned wages.

When the boys arrived with our lunch, we got straight down to eating, while listening to the records I had selected from my quite extensive collection of mostly 78 rpm singles–those heavy, brittle shellac discs that preceded the advent of vinyl. (Vinyl had been invented eight years before, back in 1948, but didn't replace shellac for singles until the early 60s.) It was in this way, at my house, that John Lennon first heard so much of the music that influenced his later musical career.

The Boy Who Became a Legend

We always ate our fish and chips and listened to my records in the lounge room at the rear of the house, overlooking the long back garden. As a rule, we preferred to stretch out on the carpet, with our backs against the chairs or the couch of the three-piece suite, rather than demurely sitting on them. Somehow this better suited the mood of our clandestine and very relaxed get-togethers. We had almost an hour of listening to music undisturbed, and enough time, if we felt like it, to play a few hands of cards before we had to tear ourselves away and cycle back up to the school. Sometimes we were late for the first lesson of the afternoon, but mostly we made it with just seconds to spare.

I had planned to give John a surprise at our lunchtime get-together that day back in 1956. However, I never dreamed it would prove to be a turning point in his life. In fact, the effect it had on him was so profound that he came to look back on it forever after as the pivotal point of his youth–the moment when he resolved to get himself a guitar and to make rock 'n' roll music his life. I had already had a great deal of influence on the shaping of John's musical tastes, and now I was about to make history as the guy who turned John Lennon onto rock 'n' roll'! When he was interviewed in 1969, after achieving phenomenal fame through the success of The Beatles, and was asked the leading question, "What was it that made you decide to become a musician?", he replied that his decision–arguably one of the most significant of all for the development of popular music in the twentieth century–was solely attributable to that lunchtime gathering at my house, and the impact on him of a newly released record that he heard for the first time that day–a record that would change everything in his life.

Little did my friend John Lennon realise, as we munched our hot fish and chips at my house that day that he was on the brink of a decision that would set the direction of the rest of his life and have an impact on popular music beyond imagining.

Front view of 69, Dovedale Road, Liverpool 18, where the author was born and grew up.

Rear back garden view. It was in the ground level lounge room, at left of the photo, that John Lennon spent many happy hours listening to records and where he recognised his musical destiny.

Chapter 2

War Infants

On another fine spring morning almost exactly ten years earlier, on 6 May 1946 to be precise, as I opened the garden gate at my home, ready to walk up Dovedale Road to school escorted by my mother, it looked like being a day much like any other I had experienced so far in my young life. What I didn't know was that I was about to meet a new boy who was joining our class that morning: a tough, talented and precocious boy named John Lennon.

As we met each other for the first time on that day in 1946, something neither of us could possibly foresee was that in almost exactly ten years' time my interest in music, so far in advance of his, would have a life-changing impact on him and, through him, on the course of modern music. But as we were only five years old when we met, this was far off in the distant and unimaginable future.

My family home was at the Rose Lane end of Dovedale Road, and, even for a five-year-old, it took only ten minutes to walk from there, across the Liverpool ring road, Queens Drive, to the school at the Penny Lane end of Dovedale Road. I was fortunate enough to live at the better end of the road: the large, semi-detached houses were set well back from the pavement behind front gardens with low wooden fences, neat privet hedges or modest walls of brick or decorative stone. All the houses had long gardens at the rear, as did those in the road behind, creating a large green expanse with plenty of light and air.

At the end I lived at, Dovedale Road was lined on both sides by wide grass verges planted with tall, slim poplar trees. The huge green double-decker corporation buses, on their route into town, turned into Dovedale Road from Rose Lane and ran past my house, before turning right into Queens Drive. At the other quieter end of Dovedale Road, between Queens Drive and Penny Lane, the houses, although still of good quality, were terraced rather than semi-detached.

I had started in the infants department at Dovedale Road County Primary School at the beginning of the school year, in August 1945, nine months before John. Since then, I had got to know most of the other boys and girls in my class, nearly all of whom had started school at the same time as me. Now, as we all settled down in the classroom on this particular May morning, the teacher introduced the newcomer to the class and told us his name was John Lennon. She also mentioned that he had recently moved to live in the nearby suburb of Woolton, which was, and still is, an area of woods, sandstone walls and old buildings, a place of relative quiet and calm.

John Lennon:

There was nothing remarkable about the new boy's appearance. He seemed of average height for his age and had light brown hair, quite neatly parted, and eyes of a similar colour. His most notable characteristics were the way he looked you directly in the eye and only rarely smiled, until he got to know and like you. It was as if he had his guard up. Joining a big class of twenty-six boys and twenty girls, who mostly knew each other well, the new boy stood out and soon made his presence felt both in the classroom and the playground.

Little John Lennon regularly misbehaved in class. Outside of the classroom he was often quite aggressive verbally, and on occasions, physically as well. The girls and the more timid boys soon learned to be wary of him. But he and I seemed to get on pretty well with each other from the start, perhaps because I was quick-witted enough to give back as good as I got and was also a lot taller than he was. We discovered that we shared a mischievous sense of humour, and that the same things, such as mimicking other children or the teachers, amused us. Lots of laughs lay ahead for us both during the years of schooling we were destined to share.

I soon learned from John that he was an only child who lived in a big house in Menlove Avenue, Woolton, not with his parents, but with an aunt and uncle. I was also intrigued by the fact that he came to school by tramcar, the number 4X, which ran along the central reservation of Menlove Avenue, then along the bottom end of Smithdown Road to the junction with Penny

Lane, where he got off. From there he walked along Penny Lane and turned left into Dovedale Road. At such a young age that was quite a big journey to get to school, compared with mine and others', and I was duly impressed.

I remember how it struck me as odd that John didn't live with his mother and father, but I don't recall him ever telling me why this was so. He did tell me that until recently he had lived with his mother in nearby Wavertree, and had previously attended Mosspits Lane County Primary School off Woolton Road.

John's Aunt Mimi accompanied him to his new school every day and, like my mother, she was there in the afternoon, standing outside the black iron railings among a gaggle of mums: no dads picked up their children in those days. Mimi seemed older than most of the other women waiting for their children, and she was always very formally dressed with a handbag, long gloves and, to the best of my recollection, a small brimless grey or fawn-coloured hat. It wasn't long after we met each other that John and I both prevailed on our 'responsible adults' to let us travel to and from school unaccompanied.

During those early days and weeks, John confided to me that he hadn't seen his mother very often since he'd gone to live with his aunt and uncle, and that she was living with another man, who was not his father. At lunchtime one day when we sat next to each other in the school canteen, I asked my new friend,

"Well John, what about your dad?" John simply replied, "Oh, he's away Mike."

I don't think his dad was ever mentioned again, either by him or by me. It was only much later that I learned the details of the unconventional and rather sad life story of John's father, Alf Lennon.

In talking to each other, John and I soon discovered that I was just a few days older than him and that we had been living quite close to each other since we were born. We had experienced the same wartime conditions that had prevailed since before we were born, and which had only recently ended.

It was in a world at war and in a city under aerial bombardment that we found ourselves when, in our own good time, we each emerged from our mother's womb in the autumn of 1940. As we got older, we learned that it was the German air force that had dropped the bombs and that their main targets had been Liverpool's ribbon of docks, with their massive warehouses, that stretched for over seven miles along the River Mersey, north and south of the city, the great Cammell Laird shipbuilding yards across the river in Birkenhead, and the factories on both sides of the river.

This whole area was known as Merseyside, and we were told that in the year before we were born, 95,000 children had, for their own safety, been separated from their families, and evacuated from Merseyside to live with families in rural areas.

But John and I remained in the city throughout the war, and were exposed to the danger of bombing. The danger was real. During the Blitz, two thirds of all Merseyside homes suffered bomb damage and almost 11,000 homes were destroyed. Both John and I were lucky that we, our families and our homes came through the bombing unscathed.

The United Kingdom had been at war with Germany since 1939, but it wasn't until 9 August 1940, shortly before we were born, that the first bombs fell on Merseyside. What a world to be born into! Three days before my birth, there had been a heavy air raid on the Liverpool docks. Two nights before John Lennon was born, high explosive bombs were dropped on the city centre and on Lichfield Road and Grantley Road in Wavertree, damaging houses only a few hundred yards away from the house in Newcastle Road where he was still nestled in his mother's womb. The following night–the night before his birth–nearby Mossley Hill, where I lived, was hit, and on the night after his birth, the city docks were again heavily bombed.

In all, there were twenty air raids on Merseyside in the month before we were born. Even so, a lot worse came in May 1941, when the full force of Hitler's *blitzkrieg* fell on Liverpool and much of the city was destroyed or heavily damaged. By the time the bombing ended in January 1942, as Hitler turned his air force on Russia, German bombing had taken a heavy toll on Merseyside, where 4,000 people had been killed and 70,000 made homeless. The loss of life and damage to property were second only to London. It was during a well-judged lull in this bombing that Julia Lennon's baby decided it was time to make its entrance into the world. Julia, then aged twenty-six, gave birth in Liverpool's Oxford Street Maternity Hospital on 9 October 1940. She named the baby boy John after his paternal grandfather, and was so inspired by Britain's wartime leader, Winston Churchill, that she also gave him the middle name of Winston.

Bomb-damaged Liverpool city centre.

9, Newcastle Road, Wavertree.

When John was born, I was just ten days old, having been born on 29 September 1940–Michaelmas Day–in the downstairs front dining room of our family house in Dovedale Road. A bed had been moved from an upstairs bedroom to the downstairs dining room in an effort to reduce the risk from potential bomb damage. Giving birth at home rather than in a hospital wasn't unusual in the 1940s, especially for second and subsequent confinements. My parents, who had been hoping for a daughter, already had a son–my brother Peter–who was nearly four years old when I was born. John Lennon, on the other hand, was his mother's first child, and was born in a hospital bed.

On the night John was born, as on many other nights, his father, Julia's husband, Alfred Lennon–always called Alf by his family–was at sea. He worked as a steward on ocean-going ships, including the *Empress of Canada,* and he was to be away from home for most of the first five years of John's life. As was the case with all merchant seamen during the war, his return visits to Liverpool were infrequent and short. By contrast, my father, Norman Hill, was in Liverpool for the duration of the war. He worked as a buyer for a telephone company, and was on emergency call as an auxiliary fireman.

While I was growing up with my brother and our parents in Dovedale Road, John Lennon, for most of the first five years of his life, lived with his mother at her father's home, 9, Newcastle Road in Wavertree, just up Church Road from Penny Lane. This was a small two-storey redbrick terraced house that stood directly on the street. It had a bay window at the front but not an inch of garden. At the back was a tiny yard. And yet, while Newcastle Road had no grass verges or trees like those in Dovedale Road and Menlove Avenue, the houses did at least have a bathroom and indoor toilet, unlike many Victorian terraced houses in Liverpool at the time.

On the other hand, there were no back gardens in which bomb shelters could be built, and the solution had been to knock together a communal one by putting a concrete roof over the alley that ran at the back of the terrace. It was to this shelter that John was carried as a baby during the night-time air raids that he and I unknowingly shared in our infancy. Whether we were blissfully unaware or somewhat traumatised is hard to say.

John and I were sixteen months old by the time the bombing stopped. Until then, I had slept under the stairs, Harry Potter style, in the tiny pantry room next to the downstairs kitchen. My cot was underneath a thick stone slab built into the walls, as this was judged to be the safest place in the house if a bomb landed on or near the building before we had time to reach the air raid shelter at the bottom of the garden. Perhaps similar precautions were taken to keep John safe at Newcastle Road.

My earliest childhood memory is of being woken from a deep slumber by the haunting wail of the air raid sirens, and of being carried, warmly wrapped, to our small sunken concrete shelter. All houses with back gardens of sufficient length were supplied with these so-called Anderson Shelters. I remember how cold and damp it was down there below the ground; but any discomfort had to be endured until the all-clear siren was sounded.

John Lennon:

Another vivid memory is of the blackout regulations, which were strictly enforced at all times. All windows had to be covered with black material so no light could escape that might help the German pilots on their night-time bombing raids; but one cold evening just before Christmas, an air raid warden hammered on our front door. From half a mile away, in Queens Drive, he had seen a sliver of light from our Christmas tree lights through a gap in the blackout lining of our front room window. Having gone to the door with my mother, I recall how upset she was to receive a stern telling-off and a ten shilling fine that we could ill afford.

This, then, was the kind of atmosphere John Lennon and I were born into and endured until we were five years old, when we met each other at last on John's first day at Dovedale Road County Primary School–the first day of what turned out to be a close friendship spanning twelve years.

Chapter 3

Traumatic Times

For a good long while, my classmates and I knew almost nothing about the unremarkable-looking boy who had stood before us for the first time one morning in May 1946, for the young John Lennon turned out to be quite reticent when it came to talking about himself. Had I been aware at the time of his troubled personal history, I might have better understood why he was sometimes such an aggressive, and not always happy, boy as we got to know each other and grew up together. But it was only much later that I came to know about, and begin to understand, the traumatic experiences he had lived through during the first five years of his life. It is clear to me now that an appreciation of the complex family circumstances of John Lennon, the child, is critical to an understanding of John Lennon, the man.

Soon after we met at Dovedale Road School, John told me he had previously been at Mosspits Lane School off Woolton Road in Wavertree. What he didn't confess (and why would he?) was that he had started in the infants there on 12 November 1945, shortly after his fifth birthday, but had been expelled for disruptive behaviour on 5 April 1946. Apparently he had been prone to bullying other children, and one particular incident, when he bullied a young girl named Pauline Hipshaw, had been the straw that broke the camel's back and resulted in his expulsion. The school authorities decided John's behavioural problems were too difficult for them to handle, and they took the drastic step of asking his mother to remove him from the school. In the discreet and somewhat disingenuous way such matters were handled, the school record noted simply that John had left the district.

All this is a far cry from the fond memories of John's cousin, Joyce. Four years older than him, and the daughter of his Uncle Sydney–his father's brother–and his Aunty Madge, Joyce remembers when four-year-old John came to live with her and her parents for an extended period of time. "He was a sweetheart, a nice boy. He was very bright and my mum idolised him. It broke her heart when he was taken away."

So John must have suffered some serious childhood agonies to turn him, in the short space of a year, from the nice little boy remembered by his cousin and idolised by his aunt, into the aggressive, disturbed child who was expelled from his first school at the tender age of five, and who I met less than six weeks later on his first day at his second school. In fact, what he had been through in this period would have disturbed the equilibrium of any child.

The Boy Who Became a Legend

From the time he and his mother, Julia, were discharged from the maternity hospital, and with his father mostly away at sea, John lived with her at the family house in Newcastle Road that was rented by his grandfather, his mother's cantankerous and domineering father, George Stanley. Also living there, until her death in 1941, were his grandmother, his mother's kind-natured Welsh mother, Annie Stanley, and one of his mother's four sisters, Anne Georgina. The eldest of his mother's sisters, Mary Elizabeth, known affectionately in the family as Mimi, lived there too, until she moved out to live with her husband, George Smith, upon his early discharge from the army in 1942.

Julia's father had been born in 1874 and was for many years a mariner in deep sea ships, having started out as a sail-maker in sailing-ships. When he'd finally had enough of being away at sea for months at a time, he got a job as a marine insurance surveyor with The Liverpool and Glasgow Salvage Association, based on the busy River Mersey. George Stanley was frequently away from home while his daughters were growing up. As his wife Annie was so kind and self-effacing, it was her strong-willed and puritanical Welsh-speaking mother, Mary Milward, who had lived with them, but died before John was born, who had the greatest influence on the strict upbringing of the five girls. It was the eldest daughter, Mimi–who would later figure so prominently in the upbringing of John Lennon–who bore the brunt of this harsh family regime, as eldest daughters often do, and it profoundly shaped her character.

John Lennon:

At the Newcastle Road house in the early 1940s, the extended female family doted on the male child, John. This made it all the more disturbing for him when he and his mother moved for a while to live on their own in a cottage at 120A Allerton Road. The cottage was near Mimi's house and was owned by her husband. According to their neighbours, John would sometimes become very anxious and upset, and would cry the house down, when he awoke in the night to find himself alone, after his mother had on occasions left him without a baby-sitter, while she went out to enjoy company in one of the nearby Woolton Village pubs.

Mother and son's move to the cottage was by no means a solitary trial for young John. He was moved around several more times in those early years, and it wasn't until he was more than five-and-a-half years old that he finally settled in the one place–at the home of his Aunt Mimi and Uncle George.

During the first four years of John's life, his father, Alf, had spent only a few weeks all told with his only child. So when Alf returned home in November 1944, after an unprecedented absence of eighteen months, he was a virtual stranger to his son. Julia had received neither money nor news from her husband for several months, and his arrival at Newcastle Road was unexpected.

While Alf was away for this extended period, Julia had an affair with a Welsh soldier, Taffy Williams, who was stationed at nearby Mossley Hill, manning an anti-aircraft unit. Julia had met Taffy while working part-time as an usherette at the Trocadero Cinema in Camden Street, off London Road in downtown Liverpool. On his return home, Alf was shocked to find his wife pregnant and to learn from her that she was expecting this man's baby. Alf magnanimously offered to rear the child as his own, but in his typically improvident way he soon returned to sea without making any practical arrangements for its upbringing.

At that time, in a family with pretensions of middle class respectability, the perceived social stigma of a child born out of wedlock was such that Julia's father brought pressure to bear on his daughter to arrange for the baby to be adopted. In this he was encouraged by his other daughters, and especially by Mimi. Wishing to keep her baby, but with nobody to support her and take her side, Julia finally succumbed to this family pressure and agreed to make the necessary arrangements both to keep the birth a secret and for the child to be adopted. Hence, on 19 June 1945, a month after the end of the Second World War, her baby daughter, whom she named Victoria Elizabeth, was born in the infirmary of a Salvation Army hostel, a mile from Newcastle Road. Julia lived there without her son, hidden from the world and especially from the eyes of prying neighbours, for several months before and a further six weeks after the birth, until the child was legally given up for adoption under a new name.

The adoptive parents of John Lennon's half-sister were a childless couple, Peder Pedersen, a thirty-eight-year-old Norwegian sailor, and his English wife, Margaret, aged twenty-five. Margaret was a regular at the cinema where Julia worked. When Julia was carrying the child, she confided to Margaret that it was to be given up for adoption. Soon after, Margaret and Peder decided to apply to become the adoptive parents.

So as to hide his mother's condition from him, before it became too obvious, and until after the baby was adopted, four-year-old John was moved by his father to Maghull, on the Liverpool outskirts, to live with his Uncle Sydney, Aunty Madge and cousin Joyce. He didn't see his mother again until he was returned to Newcastle Road eight months later, a long time in the life of a four-year-old.

Through this contrivance, and the family's silence, John grew up totally unaware of Victoria Elizabeth's existence. Contrary to most accounts–that she grew up in Norway–she in fact lived for the first eleven years of her life in Crosby in the north of Liverpool, just a few miles from where her half-brother John was living, after which she moved with her adoptive parents to the south of England. The girl wasn't told she had been adopted, and she was as much in ignorance of John's existence as he was of hers. Only in 1964, when he was aged twenty-three and newly famous as the leader of The Beatles, did John learn from one of his aunts about the birth and subsequent adoption of his half-sister. He subsequently employed an army of private detectives for two years in an unsuccessful attempt to trace his unknown sibling, and for the rest of his life he remained obsessed by his desire to contact her.

This family skeleton rattled quietly in its cupboard for more than fifty years until finally, in 1998, Lillian Ingrid Maria Pedersen, who goes by her second name, Ingrid, revealed herself to the world as John Lennon's long lost half-sister, only to disappear again soon afterwards and relapse back into obscurity. She had discovered her origins–and her relationship with one of the highest profile celebrities on earth–when she was a teenager but, as her adoptive mother had been concerned about the disruption to their lives that might ensue if the truth became public knowledge, the dutiful daughter agreed to her request that she not contact John while she, her adoptive mother, was alive. By the time her adoptive mother died, and Ingrid finally went public with her story, John had been dead for eighteen years and so, sadly, the siblings never met.

In November 1945, some four months after giving up her daughter for adoption, and with her husband once again away at sea, Julia Lennon began dating a man by the name of John Albert Dykins, a regular customer of the café in nearby Penny Lane where she now worked part-time as a waitress. This was just a month after her son had started at Mosspits Lane School. Because John was her son's name, she took to calling her new lover 'Bobby' rather than John, and the name stuck.

Their affair blossomed, and within a few months Bobby Dykins succeeded in persuading Julia's father to allow him to move into the family house in Newcastle Road to live with Julia as man and wife. At first, George Stanley hadn't been at all keen on the idea; but as he was now seventy-one years old and a widower, who had always had women to look after him, he worried that if he refused his daughter's request, she would move out of the house and he would be left on his own with nobody to care for him in his declining years. Mimi, taking the moral high ground, was pointedly critical of the proposed arrangement, but her father prevailed and Bobby moved in.

Not surprisingly, John was considered to be too young to be asked for his opinion on the matter and, again unsurprisingly perhaps, after Bobby moved in, the boy reacted angrily to this stranger who had suddenly entered his life and threatened to come between him and his mother. With her husband away for most of the time, Julia had effectively been a single mother and John hadn't been used to sharing her with anyone else. In rage and frustration, he began to behave aggressively, and took out his anger on weaker children, particularly girls. On more than one occasion he got so upset that, young as he was, he ran away from home and sought refuge at his Aunt Mimi's house. Mimi then convinced her father to pressure Julia to allow John to stay with her and her husband, until the de facto relationship between Julia and Bobby Dykins could somehow be resolved.

John witnessed some of the rows between his mother, his grandfather and his Aunt Mimi, and was only too aware of the infighting about his future that was swirling around his life. Little wonder he was upset. Sadly for him, though, things were about to get a whole lot worse.

Some weeks after Bobby Dykins moved in to live with Julia, and while John was still living at his Aunt Mimi's, Alf Lennon suddenly turned up after another long absence. Expecting, somewhat naively, to be warmly welcomed by his wife and son, he was shocked to the core to find another man living in the family home with Julia, and to learn that his only son was living at his sister-in-law's house. Julia made it patently clear to Alf that she intended to remain with Bobby come what may, at which point Alf went off to Mimi's to see John.

Shortly after this, and without informing Julia, Alf took John away from Mimi's on what turned out to be nothing more or less than an extended holiday. Father and son went together by train to stay with a friend of Alf's in Blackpool, a famous holiday resort town about 45 miles up the west coast from Liverpool. While there, Alf started to investigate the option of emigration to New Zealand with this friend and with John. How totally different John's life would have been had this option of moving to the antipodes been taken up!

After Alf and John had been away for over a month, during which they both really began to get to know each other for the first time and enjoy some happy, carefree times together, Julia managed to track them down. She arrived in Blackpool accompanied by Bobby Dykins, with the intention of taking John back to Liverpool forthwith. With Bobby waiting outside, Julia once again rejected a proposal from Alf that they try to patch up their marriage. The next issue was who was going to look after John? At this point, Alf presented his young son with a terrible dilemma. He asked the five-year-old boy to make an impossible choice: to live with his father, with whom he was getting on very well, or his mother and Bobby Dykins.

At first John elected to remain with his father but, as his mother began to take her leave, he tearfully changed his mind and ran after her instead, crying out the heartfelt words, "Mama don't go, daddy come home". He had made the gut-wrenching choice, and it seems that at this moment Alf effectively gave up on his marriage, and on being a father. Although he and Julia were never divorced and no formal custody arrangements with regard to John were ever made, Alf disappeared out of Julia's life, and out of John's as well.

Before Alf Lennon's self-exile from the family, both of John's parents and one of his aunts had been engaged in a tug of war in which he was the rope they were yanking on. But if that wasn't enough for the boy, he was about to face an even greater upset to his fragile equilibrium.

The Boy Who Became a Legend

After returning from Blackpool with his mother and Bobby Dykins, John didn't go back to his grandfather's house in Newcastle Road, nor did he go to his Aunt Mimi's. Instead, he was taken to a small one-bedroom flat that Bobby had rented for the three of them in Gateacre Village, not far from where Mimi lived. But this arrangement was to be short-lived as the issue of the custody of young John Winston Lennon came to a head.

Chapter 4

From Mummy to Mimi

John's Aunt Mimi seemed determined to gain possession of him, and in this, she succeeded. She tried to convince herself and others that her only motivation for this drastic step was to look after her nephew's best interests. However, it seems far more credible that her real motivation was to satisfy her own yearning for a child. Perhaps it was a bit of both. Either way, it was apparently at her instigation, with the support of her father–who wanted Julia back at his house so she could look after him–that a Liverpool Social Services Inspector visited Bobby and Julia's rented flat to investigate the welfare of the child.

Predictably, the inspector decreed that the living arrangements–whereby John had to share the only bedroom, and indeed the only bed, with his mother and a man who was not married to her and who was not his father–were far from satisfactory. The outcome was that Mimi was given the care of John, until Julia could arrange for him to have a bedroom of his own. Julia decided to do this by returning with Bobby Dykins to Newcastle Road, where her father was pleased to welcome her back.

At this point, just as everything appeared to have been settled, Mimi resolutely refused to hand John back to his mother and Bobby Dykins. Mimi argued that it would be much better for John if he continued to live with her and her husband at their large, comfortable house in Menlove Avenue, particularly as John had made it abundantly clear that he wasn't happy about Bobby Dykins moving into his life in place of his father. John's maternal grandfather, for his own reasons, strongly supported the case for John remaining with Mimi.

Faced with such determined pressure from her father and older sister, and still worn down, dispirited and depressed after her daughter's birth and subsequent adoption only a few months before, Julia didn't have a chance. John stayed in Mimi's care.

Thus it was that in May 1946, just before John Lennon was enrolled at Dovedale Road School and I first got to meet him, his Aunt Mimi became his de facto guardian. No legal steps were ever taken to formalise her position and that of her husband, but, as the saying goes, possession is nine-tenths of the law. From then on, it was John's Aunt Mimi, and not his mother, who took the major role in rearing him. Mimi's husband, John's kindly Uncle George, became a combination of uncle and friend to John, and the boy's source of solace whenever he incurred the displeasure of his aunt, who was a person not easily pleased.

Julia never really recovered from losing John and while Mimi put up a positive front, she carried for the rest of her life the guilt of what she had done to her sister.

As for John, after being faced with his mother taking up with a man who was a stranger to him, being expelled from school, then getting to know and like his father, only to suddenly lose him again, he now had to cope with the effective loss of his mother too–traumatic times indeed. And while he gradually adjusted to living with his aunt and uncle and settling into his new school, there can be no doubt that he deeply felt the absence of both of his parents. True, at her father's insistence, Mimi regularly took John back to Newcastle Road to visit his grandfather and his mother; but these visits dropped right off once his grandfather died in 1949, and Julia and Bobby Dykins, with their two-year-old daughter Julia, moved from the father's rented house to their own house in Allerton.

Mimi Smith, who had never had a child of her own, was already forty years old when she assumed responsibility for the rearing of her five-year-old, and behaviourally disturbed, nephew. Her self-effacing husband George was aged fifty. Before her marriage in 1939, at the age of thirty-three, to forty-three-year-old George Smith, she had been a nursing sister in charge of a ward of mental patients. And Mimi brought the strictness of her own upbringing, and the discipline of her nursing career, to bear on the raising of John. George on the other hand was easy-going, and there was never any doubt it was Mimi who ruled the household. Luckily for John, her saving grace was that she had a good sense of humour, and many a dramatic confrontation between aunt and nephew quickly turned to laughter thanks to a funny remark from John. He was always a ready wit, as we soon learned as we got to know him at school.

Mendips, the house that George and Mimi owned, was a brick-built, two-storey semi-detached, at 251, Menlove Avenue, a busy dual carriageway. It stood in the leafy suburb of Woolton, about two miles from Newcastle Road and Penny Lane. John had his own small bedroom upstairs, directly above the hall and front door. When we compared notes at school, we realised we had exactly equivalent bedrooms, small upstairs front rooms, both furnished with a single bed, a wardrobe and a small desk and chair.

Being far larger than anywhere he'd lived before, and with pleasant gardens front and back, Mendips gave John a greater degree of comfort and amenity than he'd previously enjoyed. His aunt and uncle also gave him a more stable home life and a greater feeling of security and predictability; unlike her casual and unregimented sister Julia, Mimi kept to a regular routine.

John's new house, like mine, had been built in the 1930s when people living in such houses usually employed a daily housemaid. Beyond our nearly identical bedrooms, we discovered that our houses had many similar features. One that intrigued us both as young children was the electric bell display mounted high on the wall of the kitchen/morning room. When a wall-button was pressed in one of the other rooms to summon the maid, a bell would ring and a star would revolve in the wall display, indicating the room in which the bell was being pressed. By the time John and I were growing up, there were no maids to

Mendips, John Lennon's Menlove Avenue home.

answer such a summons, and the bell systems no longer worked or had been disconnected. Just the same, ours was hardly a so-called working class upbringing, and John Lennon was neither working class nor a hero, of the type he later satirised in the song of that name.

…..John was much loved on a day-to-day basis by his dear Uncle George, who treated him more like the son he never had, than as a nephew. In her own brusque way, his Aunt Mimi loved him too. While Mimi became John's de facto mother, she never pretended to be his real one. She was always just 'Mimi' to him.

Meanwhile, although John continued to be loved by his mother, due to Mimi's active discouragement of contact with or mention of her, she gradually became a more remote person in his life as he progressed through school. In a form of role-reversal, she became more like an aunt or elder sister who he saw occasionally. After her father died and she moved to live in Allerton, he didn't see her all. Mimi had given him the impression that his mother had moved far away. It was eight months after this move that he was amazed to be shown by an older cousin, Stanley Parkes, that she in fact lived within easy walking distance of him. After that he began to visit her, behind Mimi's back, and the saying 'don't tell Mimi' became a refrain of his life.

While John got used to his new home life, his mother Julia had two daughters by Bobby Dykins–half-sisters to John. First came her namesake, Julia (now Julia Baird), born on 5 March 1947, and then Jacqueline (now Jackie Higgins), on 26 October 1949. Due to the failure of either Alf or Julia Lennon to institute divorce proceedings, Julia and Bobby were never able to marry each other, although they lived together as Mr. and Mrs. Dykins.

John told author Hunter Davies, in reference to his father, "It was as if he was dead." Alf Lennon's sister-in-law Mimi, and his wife and their family, had to all intents and purposes relegated him to the status of a non-person, as if he no longer existed.

In fact, far from being dead, Alf was very much alive. After the emotional family meeting in Blackpool in April 1946, at which he had failed to convince Julia to return to him, and in the process had lost his big chance of a relationship with his only child, Alf had returned to his seagoing life.

Some eighteen months later, while on a drunken spree in the West End of London during a shore leave, he smashed a plate glass shop front and was found by a policeman dancing in the street with a display mannequin. He had apparently been planning to go up to Liverpool to see John, but this episode cost him four months in the notorious Wormwood Scrubs Prison instead, which seems a harsh sentence for a first offence. An even more serious consequence of this misdemeanour was the loss of his seagoing career as, after he left prison, his criminal record debarred him from further employment in the Merchant Navy. With no other skill or vocation, he became an itinerant dishwasher and pot scrubber, working mostly in hotel kitchens.

The Boy Who Became a Legend

Alf had last seen his son John when the boy was five, and had had no contact with him since. He did make at least one attempt at a reunion with him, when he wrote to Mimi from prison, but she threatened, if he turned up in Liverpool, to tell John about his father being a criminal. This rebuff seems to have been sufficient to discourage Alf from any further attempts to make contact with her, Julia or John. It was only when John was aged twenty-three and had become a high profile performer with The Beatles that his father, after a lapse of eighteen years, was motivated to again make contact with him.

Deep-seated feelings of rejection and abandonment, first by his father and then so soon afterwards by his mother, haunted John throughout the remainder of his life and were all too clearly evident during the years we worked and played together at primary and secondary school. Although John managed, to some extent, to repress his sense of hurt and loss–and later to sublimate it into some wonderful songs–he remained scarred by these events and by others equally traumatic that occurred in his life before he reached manhood.

The poignant lyrics of his song "Mother" that formed part of his first post-Beatles album, *John Lennon/Plastic Ono Band* in 1970, reveal the deep and abiding pain he still felt at the age of thirty.

What a heavy load of emotional baggage five-year-old John Lennon carried with him to Dovedale Road School. The unsettling experiences of his early life left him not only insecure, but also with a distrust of people in authority that became increasingly evident as he grew up, particularly in his school life. He was left too with low self-esteem and a huge inferiority complex that he kept well hidden behind an outer shell of toughness. The hard persona he presented to the world was his way of trying to hide his vulnerability; but it remained with him always. Although he did settle down in time, it was little wonder he often behaved aggressively, particularly during our early years together in the infants.

At school, we learned enough about John to know his family circumstances were unusual, but we had no real idea of what he had experienced before he became the ward of the aunt who brought him to the school gates each morning and collected him every afternoon. He didn't have much to laugh about when he first joined our class, but I think we must have encouraged the sense of fun that tinged his life with his Uncle George and Aunt Mimi at home, and pretty soon John and his new school friends were up to a whole lot of mischief.

Chapter 5

Infants

'Bombs away!'

As John said this, his hand came down fast, karate-chop style, on the lip of the dessert spoon he had surreptitiously prepared, and both the steel spoon and its contents–a glutinous lump of tepid cabbage and potato–flew up into the air and across the crowded dining room. On this occasion the missile found its mark, landing *splat!* on the head of its hapless victim, a boy on another table who wasn't 'one of us'. The consternation caused by the accurate landing of this missile, launched from an unidentified source, gave the young missile launcher a lot of satisfaction.

From his earliest days at Dovedale Road School, John Lennon was always one of the ringleaders when it came to flicking food from one table to another during the lunchtime meal at school while the long-suffering dinner-ladies' backs were turned; and I must admit I wasn't slow in emulating his antics. Nor did it stop there. Beyond the walls of the dining room, John's warning words "Watch this Mike!" were invariably the precursor to some act of mischief or an amusing antic he was about to perform. And very often the amusement was at the expense of someone else: little boys could be nasty little pests, and John Lennon was no exception.

A particularly disagreeable type of mischief we got up to from time to time involved taking a fresh egg from our mother's pantry, and carefully carrying it to school. When we were out in the playground and had selected our victim, we crept quietly up behind him–only boys were targeted–and smashed the egg against the back of his head so that the white and the yolk rolled down his neck inside his shirt collar. Bits of the eggshell were usually matted in the boy's hair–very messy! Of course, in this rotten game it was the game itself that was rotten, not the eggs. This type of juvenile delinquency invited retaliation so you had to be vigilant lest you became a victim yourself.

Not long after John joined Dovedale Road School, we celebrated Empire Day, on 24 May 1946. After the fears, uncertainty and daily drabness of the war years, the school set out to make the celebration a big and colourful event. We were encouraged to decorate our bikes in the British national colours and to bring them to school with us. I well recall how proud I felt, as a five-year-old, cycling along the pavement of Dovedale Road and across Queens Drive from my house to the school that morning, under my mother's supervision, with my tricycle festooned with red, white and blue crepe paper and paper Union Jack flags. Others in our class did the same, but I don't remember if John was among them. I guess not, given he had to travel to school by tram. The Empire Day celebrations remained an annual event for several years–but we didn't know, and in any case wouldn't have understood, that before long there wouldn't be any Empire left for the British to celebrate.

Meanwhile, as children who had never known anything different, we accepted as normal the tedious and inconvenient rationing of everything from flour, meat, tea and sugar to newsprint, sweets and clothing, introduced during the war. By 1945, Britain emerged from the war on the winning side but bankrupt and massively in debt. After the war, only huge loans from the US and Canada kept the economy afloat. Wartime rationing not only continued after 1945; it was tightened in 1947 when the meat ration was cut and for the first time bread was rationed. Ration books were still used right up to 1954.

Many people's diet had suffered due to shortages of fresh foods, including fruit and vegetables, during five years of war, and there was particular concern for the impact on the health of the nation's children. To improve their health after the privations of wartime, all children were provided with free cod-liver oil, which we would gladly have foregone, and a small bottle of concentrated orange juice that was far more palatable. Little jars of a sweet, nutritious malt extract called Virol, which we devoured by the teaspoonful, were also provided. A tiny bottle of fresh milk, a third of a pint for each child every morning at school, completed the healthy handouts from the State. In July 1948, as the UK slowly recovered from the long and debilitating war, the modern Welfare State was introduced, providing free healthcare for all.

Schools also provided a hot cooked meal at lunchtimes–for which a small charge was made–to ensure that all schoolchildren ate at least one decent meal a day. These new 'school dinners', as they were called, included lots of vegetables, especially the aforementioned cabbage and mashed potato. Dessert was usually a stomach-filling wedge of cake with custard or, if we were lucky, semolina pudding with a dollop of jam in the middle. John Lennon was later to make use of his childhood memory of semolina when composing his nonsense song, "I Am The Walrus". Sometimes for dessert we were served tapioca pudding, which looked to us like the frogspawn we collected from ponds and took home so as to be able to watch it develop into tadpoles. All these culinary delights were served up to us children by hard-working dinner-ladies who I remember as usually being chubby and cheerful, with rosy cheeks, and, in many cases, red hands to match–though perhaps only from all that oven heat and washing up.

In our day, the infant section of the school was co-educational, whereas the junior school–which formed part of the same complex–was for boys only. Infants and juniors both had a paved playground, around the sides of which, for all the time we were there, were rectangular brick air raid shelters. Having no windows and with lights that no longer worked, these solidly built structures were very dark inside–good places for a game of hide and seek, as long as you weren't afraid of the darkness. Iron railings ran all around the school perimeter, and there were no lawns or grass playing fields.

Of course, John and I, and our immediate friends, weren't engaged in riot and mayhem all the time, and in the classroom, most of us infants settled down happily enough to a regime of play, art, music and basic learning, particularly reading and writing. In our safe, secluded environment, we were blissfully unaware of what was happening in the world around us as we laboured to learn the alphabet, spell and do our sums. While we were so occupied in the infants at Dovedale Road, many violent, momentous and bloody events were occurring out in the wider world, including the partition of India and the creation of the State of Israel.

In fine weather, when we were turned loose out of doors at playtime, the school playground could easily become a bit of a jungle, where the fittest survived and the bullies drove the weak to tears. It got worse in the junior school, in an all-male environment after the sexes had been segregated, but still there were lots of games and activities to divert us, and most children came through pretty much unscathed.

Two of the most popular and peaceful games involved rolling brightly coloured glass marbles with the aim of hitting, and thus winning, those of your opponent, and Conkers, which is played to this day with a horse-chestnut or 'conker' attached to a piece of string that has been pushed through a hole drilled in the nut and then knotted at the end. Players take turns to swing their conker as hard as they can so as to hit and smash their opponent's conker, which is held out for this purpose, dangling on its string from an outstretched arm. The player whose conker cracked and fell off its string was the loser. Old, desiccated nuts that had been soaked in vinegar usually stood up best to the rough treatment they received in the playground from the conker-wrecking ball.

We used to go off on horse-chestnut collecting expeditions, seeking good nuts to be turned into conkers. The tall horse-chestnut trees grew in some of the highest areas of Mossley Hill, not far from the church, and in some parts of Woolton, including in the grounds of Strawberry Field. The bright brown nuts, which you had to cut out of their thick, prickly bright green protective cases with a penknife, could be brought down to the ground by a well-aimed heavy stick thrown up into the branches. This may sound easy but took quite a bit of doing, and kept us amused for hours at a time.

At school, scuffles and wrestling were quite common in the playground, but only rarely led to blows. If a fight developed, a crowd quickly gathered, cheering on one or other of those rolling around on the ground. John Lennon was frequently one of the protagonists in these melees–after all, his tough-boy image had to be maintained. But mostly he was able to browbeat his opponents with his quick wit, caustic comments and choice swearwords, without needing to resort to physical force.

John took to foul language at an early age, and used it often and with relish. When he did get into a real fight, he was careful only to pick boys he reckoned he could beat, otherwise he would just hurl insults at them and run off. He and I never fought in anger, but we enjoyed a bit of friendly wrestling. Rolling around in the dirt held no fears for either of us, and we never minded getting ourselves dirty.

Name-calling was of course common among the children, and John was acutely sensitive about his middle name. Six years before, in the spring and summer of 1940, while pregnant with her first child, Julia Lennon, like most people in the UK, had been exposed to the stirring speeches of Britain's wartime leader, Winston Churchill. These motivational broadcasts on the wireless were avidly listened to in homes and pubs throughout the country and Julia was sufficiently inspired to give John the middle name of Winston. While his mother felt this to be a highly dignified name, she had unwittingly created a major problem for her son.

John came to loath the name Winston: for him, it threatened–indeed violated–a child's basic need to fit in with its peer group and not to stand out, whether by the name it is given or the clothes it is forced to wear. But John Winston Lennon was the name he was stuck with. Even years later in 1969, his attempt to rid himself of the detested name, by replacing 'Winston' with 'Ono', failed on legal grounds. All he succeeded in doing was to add 'Ono' to his name. Although from that point on he called himself John Ono Lennon, his legal name for the rest of his life was John Winston Ono Lennon, as evidenced by how his name appears in his last will and testament.

Somehow, and predictably, young J.W.L's sensitivity became generally known at school, so when John was giving someone a hard time and they wanted to get back at him, or they just wanted to wind him up and get him mad, they would chant 'Winston! Winston!' at him, or the even more hated 'Winnie', with its obvious reference to the most celebrated creation of the children's author, A.A.Milne, the bear, Winnie-the-Pooh. This provocation was guaranteed to produce an explosive reaction from John, and children who teased him in this way had to be prepared to run off fast or stand their ground and get into a wrestling match. But, no, I wasn't one of his tormentors–well, at least not as far as I remember.

Both in school and out, the suggestion "Let's pretend…" from John or any of us was a precursor to a game of make-believe. With no television, video games or the Internet, mobile phones or iPods to distract us, we were very imaginative in our play and devised our own diversions. Cowboys and Indians, and Cops and Robbers were favourite games to play in a group. If John was involved, he invariably wanted to be the leader and to have charge of assigning the roles and designing the actions, a bit like a film director. If we agreed to play Cowboys and Indians, he always insisted on being an Indian, whereas I preferred to be a cowboy as they usually won. While John preferred a bow and arrow, I loved my silver percussion-cap six-shooter pistol that had its own holster on a low-slung belt.

So much make-believe play stimulated our imagination. Combined with the stories that were read to us as small children and later with the love of reading that John and I both developed, it proved to be a rich and deep resource on which the older John Lennon drew in both his song writing and writing for the page. "My Uncle George reads me a story or two every night at bedtime" he once told me at the beginning of a reading session in the classroom. I replied that my mum did the same for me.

Of course, not all was sweetness and light at school. Misbehaviour, even by the little kids in the infants, risked sharp retribution in the form of corporal punishment. We weren't introduced to the deterrent of the bamboo cane until we progressed to the junior school; in the infants, the punishment usually took the form of a sharp slap, with the flat of the teacher's open hand, on the child's bare thigh. These days, such measures would land a teacher in serious trouble, but back then the headmistress of the infant school, a Miss Wooley, was a particular terror when it came to this simple but effective form of public humiliation–public, because it was usually administered in front of your class, with one hand pushing up the girl's skirt or the leg of the boy's shorts and the other delivering the slap.

For children who had never been slapped like this before, the first time usually came as an enormously shocking experience that produced a flood of tears and, perhaps some psychological damage along with the tears and sore red skin. I well remember the experience myself, although it was not entirely novel since my father sometimes smacked me on the bare bottom in my bedroom when sufficiently exasperated by some bad behaviour on my part–perhaps refusing to eat my vegetables during Sunday lunch! John, too, received plenty of corporal punishment during his schooling, but always accepted it with stoicism. I don't believe his Aunt Mimi ever physically punished him at home, and gentle Uncle George could never have brought himself to strike his much loved nephew.

In those days, all British boys of primary school age wore short pants, on or above the knee in length, in and out of school and all year round, even on cold and frosty winter mornings. Hardwearing velvet-corduroy shorts with white cotton linings were commonly worn, especially in cooler weather. There were no denim clothes and no jeans. Boys didn't normally wear long pants or trousers before the age of twelve or thirteen, depending on their height; but when the transition from shorts to longs was finally made, it marked a significant milestone in a boy's development, after which he would rarely wear shorts again, except on the playing field or as a part of a Boy Scout uniform.

Author aged 8 (at right) using typical 'S' clasp belt.

As evidenced by most photos of boys taken in this period, we all seemed to hold up our shorts with the same type of elasticised black and yellow striped fabric belt with a metal snake clasp in the shape of the letter 'S'. I know both John and I did.

Wearing short-shorts as we did in all types of weather, we often had cold knees. During our second winter in the infants at Dovedale Road School in 1946-47, our knees were especially cold. In terms of low temperatures, blizzards and snowfall, it was the worst English winter on record. I can hear John even now coming out with one of his choice comments such as "Fuckin' hell, it's cold enough to freeze the balls off a brass monkey." The whole country, including Merseyside, was buried under snow and ice for weeks on end.

In our homes the water pipes froze, which meant no running water from the taps for several days. Then, when the thaw came, some of the water pipes in the attic burst and water dripped through the plaster of the ceilings into the rooms below. Buckets and bowls were strategically placed in an attempt–that was only ever partly successful–to catch the overflow, until a hard-pressed plumber arrived to repair the leaks.

As very few British houses had central heating, people coped as best they could during cold spells. Mine certainly didn't have this modern 'luxury', and neither did John's. I remember us comparing notes on how cold our houses were as we shivered in the school playground early one particularly cold winter's morning. We both went to bed on cold nights with a rubber hot water bottle, and we had the same experience of getting out of bed on a cold winter's morning to find that ice had formed during the night on the *inside* of our bedroom windows, and to such an extent that we couldn't see out through the glass into the street. We also both got frozen feet from standing on cold linoleum or tiled floors in the toilet or bathroom, when, as often happened, we forgot–or couldn't be bothered–to wear our slippers.

In that era, most houses were heated by a coal-burning fire in the downstairs lounge room and gas fires in some of the other rooms. The coal fire was either allowed to go out by itself at night or was damped down with slack–fine coal dust. My house had been built with an open fireplace in the front dining room, as well as the lounge, and in both the larger upstairs bedrooms. But since there were no longer any maids to carry coal scuttles upstairs or to clean the ashes from the grates and re-lay the fires, these had all been converted to gas burning. Some houses had a freestanding oil heater in the front hall as well, but again this was usually turned off at bedtime.

Hardly any houses were fitted with walk-in showers, and most people made do with a daily stand-up wash at a basin, and a weekly hot bath. At least this was an improvement on medieval times when, so we were amused to learn at school, men traditionally bathed only twice a year, at Easter and Michaelmas. I always remembered this amusing piece of trivia, as Michaelmas Day, 29 September, is my birthday.

Those cold winters, with night frosts that turned the thawing snow to ice, were when children made long ice slides on the pavements, and at school. Every winter, we had some great ice slides in the school playground, on which the more daring or reckless children reached high speeds on the slippery polished surface in their leather-soled shoes–no one wore the equivalent of sneakers or trainers to school in those days. This was the kind of weather in which the young John Lennon wore a woollen Balaclava helmet back to front for greater effect. He always liked to be noticed and recognised as the gang leader he aspired to be.

Liverpool, in the northwest of England, didn't normally get as much snow as the south and east of the country, but, when enough did fall, we thoroughly enjoyed tobogganing down steep slopes. John was as much of a daredevil when it came to tobogganing as he was at skating on the ice slides. Amazingly, neither of us ever broke any bones, and didn't suffer anything worse than grazed knees and wet and dirty clothes.

One day at school, in the entrance of one of the disused brick air raid shelters where we liked to meet, John and I got into a discussion about the pets we had at home. "We've got two cats and a dog at home that belong to my aunt and uncle," he said. "Then I have my own cat called Tim that I had found as a stray kitten and Mimi let me keep".

I replied, "Gosh–that's a lot of animals. I can't match that. There's only one cat in my house, a jet-black one named Smutty, that we've had that since he was a little kitten". Then I had John in hysterics as I told him the story of how, when I was very young, I stuffed Smutty up a long drainpipe at the side of our house. I had been impressed by how cats could climb up vertical tree trunks, and was curious to see if my little cat could climb all the way up the inside of a two-storey metal drainpipe. I kept pushing Smutty in and up, hoping to see his head appear out of the top of the pipe at the roof of the house. Fortunately for the kitten, my mother caught me in the act and put a stop to the experiment. When I was older, the family teased me about how as a child I had used up several of the cat's supposed nine lives. But I became very fond of him in the same way as John did of Tim. Although John could be cruel to people, he never was to animals.

John also liked my tale of how my cat fancied himself as a big game hunter. I told him how Smutty had finished off my older brother's large family of white mice when it had hidden itself and been locked up overnight in the laundry, where the mice were kept in a box; how it had killed a budgerigar that had escaped from its cage; and how my brother and I quite regularly had to undertake the unpleasant task of drowning, in a bucket of water, half-dead birds that the cat had expertly stalked and pounced upon, on the back garden lawn.

In the classroom John could sometimes get bored, and then he would go looking for mischief as a diversion. But, as we gradually worked our way up through the school grades, he displayed interest and ability in reading, writing and art. His artistic efforts were quite often displayed around the school, which is more than can be said for mine.

We both took to reading for pleasure at a relatively early age in those pre-television days. John's Aunt Mimi had lots of good books at home and had a regular supply of new ones through the book club to which she subscribed. She and Uncle George were both keen readers and they passed on their enthusiasm to their nephew.

After the war ended, George became and remained unemployed, apart from an abortive loss-making effort working from home as an illegal off-course bookmaker. This business failure left him with no income apart from the rents on some cottages he had inherited from his father. He became a fixture at home, reading in his favourite armchair and he was thus able to devote a lot of time to his young nephew. Mimi took in a lodger to bring in some much needed income.

John was encouraged and allowed to read anything that took his fancy, including books that most adults would have regarded as too advanced for his age group. This helped to give him an impressive vocabulary well in advance of most of his contemporaries. It stood him in good stead in later life when he used it to great effect in his song writing. And even earlier, when John was very young, Uncle George used to sit him on his knee and teach him new words by reading to him from the local newspaper, the *Liverpool Echo*. This seems to be what gave John a lifetime fondness for reading newspapers, which he referred to in the song, "A Day in The Life".

All in all, John found the written word a marvellous form of escape from the stress of his family life. The private world of the imagination, into which he retreated at school age through reading, writing, drawing, colouring and painting, provided him with stimulus, as well as a feeling of safety and comfort.

Chapter 6

Neighbourhood Life

Although John and I made some good friends at school, we both had friendships too with boys who went to different schools, but lived in the same neighbourhood. This was especially the case with John, as most of the friends who lived near him in Woolton attended Springwood Primary School in Allerton, or Mosspits Lane Primary School, where he had started his schooling before he was expelled and began again at Dovedale Road School. After he moved to live in Woolton, it didn't take John long to make his presence felt in his new neighbourhood, even while he was still at infant school.

John's new Woolton friends included the boy who later became his closest childhood friend, Pete Shotton. Pete lived in Vale Road, just behind John's house: he had an unusually pink complexion and a head of natural, almost white, curls. In due course Pete and I became good friends too. With Pete being ten months younger than John, by the time he started at Mosspits Lane School, John had already left there and had moved to Dovedale Road School. The pair actually met at the Sunday school at St. Peter's Parish Church in Woolton that John attended every Sunday afternoon from the age of seven. John and Pete didn't attend school together until they started at the same grammar school at the age of eleven.

Outside primary school, though, Lennon and Shotton became almost inseparable, like a pair of terrible twins, and this closeness extended to school life once they started together at Quarry Bank. Looking back at the beginning of their childhood friendship, Pete Shotton recalled, in the candid and entertaining book he was motivated to write by John's murder in 1980, *John Lennon–In My Life*, how 'this sandy-haired kid with the ridiculous glasses proved, almost from the start, to be what our parents would have labelled "a disruptive influence". Not only was he larger, stronger and more aggressive than the rest of us, he also seemed a lot wiser to the ways of the big bad world.'

Those 'ridiculous round glasses' were the simple round wire-frame type provided free of charge by the new National Health Service and known simply as 'National Health specs'. John's defective eyesight was identified when he was seven, and was apparently a weakness inherited from his mother.

The more he was teased for wearing glasses, the more sensitive he became about being seen with them on. So he increasingly left off wearing them in public, and especially at school. And besides the teasing, the face-furniture didn't at all suit the tough-boy image he liked to project. He preferred to be handicapped and half-blind rather than to compromise in the style department.

The Boy Who Became a Legend

It is ironic then, that, as every Lennon t-shirt and poster from here to kingdom come shows us, twenty years later, in 1966, when John was a star on both sides of the Atlantic, he took up the habit of wearing the same kind of plain round thin-framed 'granny' glasses. People came to associate these old-style glasses so much with him that they became his globally recognised trademark. Perhaps his fame insulated him from the derisory comments from others that had so stung him in childhood or maybe he just took a perverse delight in doing as an adult something he had abhorred doing as a child. Whatever the impulse was, he remained averse to wearing glasses while performing on stage, and used contact lenses instead.

Another young Woolton friend of John's who didn't go to the same primary school as us was Nigel Walley who lived, like Pete Shotton, in Vale Road. As was the case with Pete, Nigel attended Sunday school with John, and at the age of sixteen he became the first manager of John's Quarry Men group, which after many vicissitudes, eventually developed into The Beatles. Also attending that Sunday school was Rod Davis, who later went to the same grammar school as me and John and who at the age of fifteen joined the embryonic group as a banjo player, with John and Eric Griffiths, both of whom were trying to learn to play guitars.

Last, but not least, there was Ivan Vaughan, another Woolton friend of John's but one who was also a school friend of ours at Dovedale Road School, despite being in the academic year below us. Like Pete Shotton and Nigel Walley, Ivan lived in Vale Road. His house was directly behind John's and they were able to chat over the back garden fence. This was how they had met, soon after John moved to live at Woolton, and they became firm friends.

Ivan's contribution to John Lennon's life and to the development of rock and pop music was to be very significant, although none of us could have envisaged this when we were all school friends together in the 1940s. It was Ivan Vaughan's destiny, in July 1957, to open the way for one of the most productive and successful musical partnerships, by persuading his guitar-playing and musically precocious friend at the Liverpool Institute High School, a boy by the name of Paul McCartney, to accompany him to the fete at St. Peter's Parish Church in Woolton, where The Quarry Men were performing, and then introducing him to his old friend John Lennon. The rest, as they say, is history.

Also at Dovedale Road School from 1947, two years below us and thus one year below Ivan Vaughan, was a quiet little five-year-old boy who none of us knew at the time. This boy's whole life was later to be fundamentally affected by his progression, at the age of eleven, like Ivan Vaughan a year before him, to the Liverpool Institute, where, through their common interest in guitar playing, he became friends with Paul McCartney, a boy in the school year above him. The name of this quiet boy was, of course, George Harrison.

The Boy Who Became a Legend

At about the same time that George Harrison started at Dovedale Road School, John Lennon met Pete Shotton, and, after assuming the leadership of Pete's group of friends, proceeded to lead them all astray. Before long, Lennon's gang, as it became known, achieved notoriety for mischief and mayhem in and around Woolton and Allerton. One of the members of this little gang, David Ashton, recalled that "John was alluring and beguiling, even bewitching to be with or near, sometimes even spellbinding, but never boring. There were lots of kids banned by their parents from playing with his gang but we played anyway."

A glimpse, through our infant eyes, of neighbourhood life in south Liverpool in the years immediately following the Second World War, may provide a better understanding of what it was like for John Lennon and his friends to be growing up then. Although we were living in a city, both John and I were exposed to a similar village type of lifestyle in our nearby leafy suburbs of Woolton and Mossley Hill. Both had been villages in their own right before being absorbed by the spread of suburbia in the 1930s.

In those days, when few people drove cars and there were no shopping malls, a wide range of goods and services were delivered to people in their own homes. These home deliveries included the regular early morning milk, the mail–two deliveries daily, in the morning and the afternoon–and the weekly rubbish collection. On request, there were also deliveries by the baker and by the coal merchant, who lugged huge, heavy sacks of coal on his leather-padded shoulders and dumped them in his customer's own coal stores. I well recall too the ever-cheerful and hardworking window cleaner, Mr. Wicks, who came to us fortnightly in all weathers wearing just a shirt, with the sleeves rolled up, and no jacket. He was the man who had six or seven daughters before he was finally blessed with a son who he was looking forward to taking with him to Anfield, when he was old enough, to see Liverpool Football Club play soccer. Finally, about once a month, a barber would be in our neighbourhood, cutting the hair of an entire family—or the children at least—in their own home.

Unscheduled callers included knife and garden tool sharpeners with a mobile grinding wheel, sellers of Spanish onions, rag-and-bone men crying out loudly, "Any old iron? Any old iron?" just like the eponymous music-hall song, gypsy fortune-tellers and door-to-door salesman peddling anything from vacuum cleaners to encyclopedias. To us as young children, this was a varied pageant, and full of interest.

It seems extraordinary now, but many of these deliveries came by horse and cart. This gave rise to hot competition among neighbours to be the first to rush out into the road with a small brush and pan to collect the still steaming horse-droppings, so prized for nurturing roses and vegetables in the garden. You had to be quick off the mark as soon as the approaching *clip clop* of a horse's hooves was heard. I made

John laugh one time by telling him how adept and unembarrassed my mother was at collecting horseshit from the middle of the road, to which he replied "Christ Mike–my aunt wouldn't be seen dead doing anything like that!"

A couple of minutes' walk from my house, in the opposite direction to Penny Lane, brought you to Rose Lane, across which to the left was a little street, Rose Brae, where there was a working dairy. A peep in there at milking time was a revelation of strange sights and smells. Besides the cows in their stalls, there was a huge carthorse. John's Uncle George had been a dairyman, working for his father, and as a young child, John had been thrilled to be taken out on his milk cart. The business was sold during the war after the father died.

These small independent dairies were a feature of the suburbs; the milk they produced came in glass bottles with cardboard tops, and the rich full cream sat in the neck of the bottle. With most homes not yet equipped with refrigerators, daily deliveries of fresh milk were important.

Denise Eaves, nee Wickens, was my childhood girl-next-door, at 67, Dovedale Road. Denise now lives in Vancouver, and she reminded me, when we met in that city recently, that in Rose Lane, close to the dairy and next to Rose Lane School, which has since been demolished and replaced by a Tesco supermarket, was a popular sweetshop with the emotive name of Aunt Lollipops, which did a brisk trade with schoolchildren and may well, I think, twenty years later, have influenced John Lennon's choice of imagery in the verse of the wonderfully psychedelic "Lucy in the Sky with Diamonds".

Turning right from Dovedale Road into Rose Lane took you towards Mossley Hill Village, past Bookocks Newsagent and Tobacconist, which John Lennon always referred to as 'Newsagent and Tobogganist'. My brother and I used to turn up there weekly with a few pennies and coupons from the family ration book to buy our meagre allowance of sweets, which were still rationed due to restrictions on sugar imports. This was the same shop where, in our teenage years, when John came regularly to my house at lunchtimes to listen to my records, he would often buy a few cigarettes.

In Mossley Hill Village proper, on the opposite side of the road, was the little post office, run for years by the man who for generations was the leader of the wolf cub pack that met further up the hill of Rose Lane towards beautiful Mossley Hill Church, which at the time was bomb-damaged and still awaiting repair.

Just along the road at the foot of the hill was the local Co-op store where our family bought its groceries. Such stores were the equivalent of today's supermarkets, and there was one in Woolton too, which contained the same feature that fascinated John and me as children. This was the contraption involved in paying for what you had bought and receiving your change.

The way it worked, was the shop assistant took the cash from the customer, screwed it inside a small metal cylinder along with an adding machine's tally of the purchases, and attached the cylinder to a pulley apparatus worked by springs. When the assistant pulled a lever, the mechanism carried the cylinder high up on an overhead wire to a glass-sided booth that had similar wires converging on it from all parts of the store. There, a lady cashier took out your money, replaced it with the correct change, screwed the cylinder tightly closed, and sent it winging its way back to the counter and the patiently waiting customer. This Heath Robinson-like apparatus was a far cry from today's computerised checkouts and barcode readers, but much more interesting to children. We never tired of watching the metal cylinders whizzing along the network of overhead wires far above our heads.

Past the Co-op and up the hill over the railway line up to town or down to Garston and Speke, was Mossley Hill Station. On the way up this hill on the right-hand side was the fish and chip shop, where it was a real treat to have four penny worth of hot potato chips and a small bottle of ginger beer. There was also the chandler's shop full of strong evocative smells such as paraffin and creosote, and an eclectic range of items, from sticky flypapers to boot polish. My mother told me they were even reputed to sell elbow grease! And then there was the Chinese laundry, with its smells of carbolic soap and clouds of steam, run by a hard-working and traditionally-dressed Chinese family. To us, as young children, these very short and strangely-dressed people with pigtails seemed almost like creatures from another planet.

Behind the houses opposite mine in Dovedale Road was a grassed rectangular park. In summer we were fond of starting small fires in the long dry grass. The grass used to burn nicely and produced quite a lot of smoke. This sometimes excited a few of the nearby householders, but we thought it was fun. To my knowledge there was never any property damage although there could well have been some smoky washing on clotheslines.

Another misdemeanour of mine when I was still an infant was when I allowed myself to be egged on by my ten-year-old brother and his mates to do something none of them had the courage to do. This was to strike a match and set light to the thick, dry brushwood at the far end of our long back garden–a thicket so dense that you couldn't see into the garden behind. Well, the deed was soon done. It took only a single match and there was a huge if short-lived blaze. By the time the fire had died down, you could walk between the two gardens: both brushwood and wooden fence had gone. We too were gone–from behind the garden shed where we had been cowering–the moment we heard the sound of an approaching fire engine, presumably called by a neighbour! Punishment came later.

Responding to a dare was always a good way for a child to build up its status in a group, but it was also the cause of no end of juvenile mischief. John wasn't involved in this particular act of arson, but I remember him being very impressed when I gave him a graphic account of it at school the next day.

John Lennon, aged seven, is in the back row, the 8th boy from the left of the photo. The author is the tallest boy in the photo, 11th from the left. Note the air raid shelter behind the children.

By June of 1948, as we neared the end of our third and final year in the infants at Dovedale Road School, John's disruptive behaviour, at least in class, had calmed down a good deal and we were both doing quite well academically. Before the boys moved up into the junior school and the girls moved out to other girls-only schools, we had a group photo taken of all the children in our class–the only one taken during our years in the infants. In this photo of the seven-year-old boys and girls, I can be seen towering above all the other children–the tallest child in the infants. John Lennon, without his glasses, can also clearly be seen in this now extremely rare photo.

With our move across from the co-educational infants at Dovedale Road School, John and I began four years together in the juniors, to be followed by a further five at grammar school, all in a male-only environment. During those nine years, and especially for those of us without sisters of a similar age, girls were to become strange and remote creatures to be shunned until we were well into our teenage years.

Looking back at our early years together in the infants at Dovedale Road School, I see that John Lennon and I were well positioned to become, if not partners in crime, then at least partners in fooling around. We had plenty more of that to look forward to.

John (top left) and the author (top right).

Chapter 7

Junior School

Boys were zooming this way and that, zigzagging across the playground, running as if their lives depended on it, their arms pumping like pistons, then, if cornered, doubling over with hands spread out in front of them in an effort to protect their genitals. They were playing the most popular extracurricular game in the junior school–the noble sport of ball-tick, a particular variety of tag at which John Lennon was highly proficient. In our vernacular, tag was always referred to as tick, and the balls in this game were testicles. The object was to chase and catch another boy, then to grab his testicles, whereupon he became 'it' and had to do the chasing. I guess this peculiar form of tag was indicative of an increased awareness of our developing sexuality.

Before being initiated in such new playground games, John and I had felt very grown-up as we started together in the juniors at Dovedale Road School on 25 August 1948, although we were not quite eight years old. Having shed all the girls with whom we had shared the last three years in the infants, we had been joined in the juniors by boys who had been at other infant schools. These included Tim Holmes and Don Beattie, both of whom, in time, became our good friends. Another boy, Jimmy Tarbuck, who had already gained a reputation around the neighbourhood for fighting and mischief, had joined us in the infants in May 1948. He had previously attended a nearby private school, and I suspect that, like John Lennon, he had had to leave there because of misbehaviour. Although later he too became one of my friends, he and John soon became rivals as school tough kids at Dovedale Road School.

The school encouraged the wearing of a school uniform, although this wasn't expected in warm summer weather. The uniform was comprised of a black blazer with a green breast badge, a school tie and a school cap, that also had a badge.

As well as being allocated to a class comprising boys in the same age group, all boys were allocated to one of the four school houses under the banner of which they participated in non-academic activities, principally sport. The houses were named Clive, Drake, Nelson and Wolfe: all heroes of the British Empire. There were also school monitors and a host of new things to get used to.

The author aged 10 in Dovedale Road School blazer.

The Boy Who Became a Legend

The school motto was 'Kindness, Courtesy and Consideration for others', and the teachers tried hard to instil these virtues into the children, with varying degrees of success.

There were changes in school games too. In the warmer weather, we now played cricket and lots of rounders. This was a baseball-style game, but played with a soft ball and a smaller bat with a flat surface, rather like a small cricket bat.

Teaching the boys to swim was part of the school curriculum from about the age of ten, and as the school didn't have its own pool, we were taken once a week during the winter to the Picton Road Baths, a none too hygienic municipal indoor swimming pool. We had a long walk to get there and back, often through rain, sleet and snow, carrying a towel and our woollen bathing costumes–or "cossies", as we called our swimming trunks–across busy Smithdown Road and through an extensive park, Wavertree Playground, always referred to as "The Mystery." This unusual name derived from the mystery of the anonymous benefactor who purchased the land in 1895 and donated it to the city for use as a park on the condition his name was never to be revealed. The mystery remained until just a few years ago in Liverpool when the benefactor was finally identified as Philip Holt, a local Victorian shipowner and philanthropist. Who knows, perhaps this was the remote origin of the name of The Beatles' *Magical Mystery Tour*?

John Lennon:

After nearly drowning on one occasion in the deep end of the swimming pool, and at the cost of picking up one of the all too common ear infections, that later necessitated two operations in hospital and left my hearing permanently impaired, both John Lennon and I were awarded our twenty-five yards swimming certificates. John managed to achieve his with no apparent ill effects. Swimming was really the only form of physical exercise he enjoyed and did well at, although he quite enjoyed cycling. He was never enthusiastic about team sports like football for a reason that he was always reluctant to acknowledge–he literally couldn't keep his eye on the ball and couldn't see well enough to participate, unless he wore his glasses, which, as we have noted, he was always loath to do in public.

By today's standards our school classes were large–over forty boys–but, as I recall, classroom conditions weren't too chaotic. Order was generally well maintained by the mostly male teaching staff, of whom several had served in the armed forces and knew something about discipline. The cane was used effectively–one hard whack on the palm of an outstretched hand in front of the class really hurt, and went on stinging for quite a while. It helped, at least for a time, to keep in line class troublemakers and potential juvenile delinquents, John Lennon and myself included.

Mostly we enjoyed the lessons and managed to acquire some learning. In fact, we came to enjoy classes so much that we became far less disruptive. We were fortunate to have good teachers. Besides English language, literature and arithmetic–the multiplication tables were really drummed into us–we started to learn some history and geography, as well as elementary science.

John showed real interest in, and promise at, art. He enjoyed drawing and painting and, during his years at Dovedale Road School, was awarded several art prizes. One prize he was especially pleased to win was a book entitled *How to Draw Horses*. Besides producing recognisable and amusing caricatures of fellow-pupils or teachers, John became fond of drawing cripples, dwarfs and grotesque figures, emphasising physical deformities or afflictions, such as twisted limbs, warts and sores. When we were aged ten or eleven, I can remember countless times looking over his shoulder while he was sitting at the desk drawing, and seeing some hunchback or dwarf leering up at me from the page–the type of cartoon figures in which he increasingly specialised. By the time he became a teenager, he had refined these distorted images into a very personal art form.

Hunchbacks had held a particular fascination for John since we had seen the memorable 1939 motion picture film of Victor Hugo's classic novel, *The Hunchback of Notre Dame*. One of John's party pieces, in and out of the classroom, was a hilarious take off of Charles Laughton's portrayal in this film of the tragic figure of Quasimodo, complete with twisted arm and body, shambling gait and insane grin. When he became a musician, he even amused himself on occasions by including such take offs in his stage performances.

The total lack of sensitivity and compassion shown by John towards the mentally and physically handicapped might have gone down well in the Hitler Youth, but it shocked even the often-insensitive Liverpudlians. We weren't easily embarrassed but there were times, while we were walking along a street with John, that one of his sudden leering hunchback performances, in front of some unfortunate Down's syndrome or physically handicapped boy who was passing by, had us wishing we weren't with him. His way of handling exposure to such abnormalities was often to laugh, even in the presence of those afflicted, and with total disregard for their feelings; but sometimes, when brought face to face with serious deformity, he was revolted, and would turn away or even flee if he could. This unfortunate personality trait illustrates the Jekyll & Hyde nature of his character and has never been satisfactorily explained–a job for a psychiatrist perhaps? Maybe in some subliminal way, he felt he too was handicapped, but on the inside, through the personal anguish he had endured, and he tried to use his art as a way of alluding to, and making fun of, his own suffering.

This sick and insensitive form of humour, reflected in his art and his behaviour, was in contrast with his otherwise innate generosity of spirit. It was as if the sensitivity, compassion and understanding, that in the human race has suppressed and replaced the primeval animal urge to ridicule and shun any abnormal member of a species, was somehow missing or burnt out in John's makeup. His sick humour was often seriously sick.

On a lighter note, John's fascination with English words used in amusing ways developed as he progressed through junior school. We were both fond of nonsense poems such as Edward Lear's *The Owl and the Pussycat*.

Among our favourites was:

One fine day in the middle of the night,
Two dead men got up to fight.
Back to back they faced each other,
Drew their swords and shot each other.

Another favourite was the simple classic that appealed to our juvenile sense of humour:

In days of old
When knights were bold
And lavatories weren't invented,
They dropped their load
In the middle of the road
And went away contented.

There were plenty of juvenile jokes in circulation too, and John always seemed to have a few of them to trot out, especially of the smutty variety. On the other hand, some of his jokes were

John Lennon:

clean and of Christmas cracker quality. One I can still recall to this day is:

Question: What is yellow and dangerous?

Answer: Shark-infested custard.

In retrospect, given what lay ahead for him, it is surprising that John showed no particular interest in, or aptitude for, music at school, but we were taught a wide variety of songs that we sang together in class to the accompaniment of a piano played by one of the teachers. One of our favourites was the Negro spiritual, "Swing Low Sweet Chariot". Others included "D'ye Ken John Peel", "Widdecombe Fair" and "Dashing Away With the Smoothing Iron (she stole my heart away)".

We also enjoyed having stories read to us in class. The teacher always chose a story judged likely, when read as a serial, to hold the attention of a class of restless young boys. A chapter or two at a time was read to us, and we usually looked forward keenly to the next episode. One we especially enjoyed hearing read to us in this way was John Buchan's novel *The Thirty-Nine Steps*. Others were Arthur Conan Doyle's *The Lost World* and Sir H. Rider Haggard's *King Solomon's Mines*.

In our quieter times at home, curled up on the settee or in bed, John and I shared a love of reading for pleasure. This had been encouraged in his case by his Uncle George who had read to him from books and newspapers since he was a five-year-old and first came to live with his aunt and uncle. John was particularly taken with Richmal Crompton's series of *Just William* books. The mischievous eleven-year-old schoolboy, William Brown, with his gang called The Outlaws, served as a role model for John who, just like William, was frequently up to mischief and was the leader of his own little neighbourhood gang.

We both enjoyed the amazing adventures of Alice in Lewis Carroll's *Alice's Adventures in Wonderland* and *Through the Looking-Glass*. With his fondness for nonsense poetry and the odd use of words, John was especially taken with Lewis Carroll's *Jabberwocky* and *The Walrus and the Carpenter*. The influence of these in his later books and song lyrics is quite apparent.

We also enjoyed such classics as Kenneth Grahame's *The Wind in the Willows,* Robert Louis Stevenson's *Treasure Island* and *Kidnapped,* and Daniel Defoe's *Robinson Crusoe.* In an interview with journalist Pete Hamill, published in *Rolling Stone Magazine* on 5 June 1975, John referred to *The Wind in the Willows, Alice in Wonderland* and *Treasure Island* as "the books that really opened my whole being at age seven and eight."

Many of us had parties at home for our birthdays, and my good friend, Tim Holmes, kindly shared with me recently his recollections of John Lennon attending his ninth or tenth birthday party. "At the end of my party, we were all playing in the house with a small wooden cart belonging to my brother. John sat astride this thing convinced he was a duck. Nothing would make him stand up and go home. He was pushing himself up and down the hallway, calling out over and over 'I'm a duck. Leave me alone. I'm going to lay an egg.' His quacking noises were really lifelike, and his antics were hilariously funny."

Bob Hayes, a friend who had been with John and me in the infants at Dovedale Road, also has childhood birthday party memories of John Lennon. John was one of the guests at Bob's tenth birthday party during which he and Bob got into a wrestling match. John had Bob pinned down on the lounge room carpet when Bob, determined not to be bested by John in a fight in his own house and drawing on hidden reserves of strength, suddenly gave a great push upwards, heaving John up and over with the consequence that John banged his head against a thick glass sliding door so hard that he cracked the glass pane. John took it all in his stride, simply saying to Bob "Gosh, you're strong aren't you", and not worrying about his sore head. Bob's mother didn't take it quite so calmly when she discovered the damage.

Chapter 8

Entertainment

From May 1951, when we were both aged ten, the weekly *Goon Show* on the wireless (we never called it the radio in those days), starring Peter Sellers, Spike Milligan and Harry Secombe, became a good source of zany humour. We continued to enjoy listening to this comedy show right through our grammar school days, avidly following the manic adventures of a host of characters such as Neddie Seagoon, Eccles, Bluebottle and Major Bloodnok, and discussing them next day in school. We often used to try to mimic their crazy accents and characteristics. We also liked the strip cartoon *Curly Wee and Gussie Goose* in the *Liverpool Echo*; happy memories that we shared.

The weekly comics that were delivered to our homes along with the daily newspapers were eagerly awaited on delivery day. We pounced on these the moment the paper delivery boy pushed the newspaper through the front door letterbox and we heard it land '*flop*' on the hall floor. My favourite comic was the *Eagle*, and I was hooked on this from the first edition in October 1950. I particularly loved the science fiction serial on the front page that featured Dan Dare, Pilot of the Future, doing

John Lennon:

battle against his arch-enemy, the Mekon, with his huge bald green head filled with evil intentions.

The Eagle comic.

At John's home, Mimi took a dim view of comics. They weren't the sort of reading she favoured for him. *Eagle* was the only comic she grudgingly allowed into the house, perhaps because it was edited by a clergyman. But John told me his Uncle George sometimes smuggled other comics in for him to read surreptitiously. These might include the *Dandy* and *Beano* that were taken to school to be keenly read from cover to cover and then swapped for other comics. These weekly comics also came out as hardback annuals. They made welcome Christmas and birthday presents, at least in my house, as did *Rupert* books and annuals.

As we progressed through school, most of us took up hobbies and especially collecting–everything from train numbers to colourful cigarette packets. The best place for us to get discarded cigarette packets was the Prince Alfred Road tram and bus depot off Church Road, just up from Penny Lane, and very near where John used to live in Newcastle Road. There, emulating his literary hero, William Brown of *Just William* fame, John loved to get dirty and smelly as we and other boys fossicked through the mounds of garbage swept up by the bus and tram-cleaning staff, keenly searching for less common cigarette packets, such as Passing Cloud and exotic foreign brands. Rare matchboxes also turned up and could be swapped with others who collected them. These were the days when most men and some women smoked, and when people were allowed to smoke on the top deck of trams and buses.

Both John and I also took up the more educational hobby of stamp collecting, although he soon lost interest and didn't build up much of a collection. We bought some stamps from dealers who mailed little books of stamps to our homes on approval. We also swapped and traded stamps with other collectors at school. I went to stamp fairs too, and sometimes went on my own to the homes of elderly men I met at them, who were augmenting their pensions by selling off their collections, stamp by stamp. Nowadays, parents would probably be concerned lest anything untoward was on the agenda of such unaccompanied home visits, but people were more trusting then. Apart from an occasional hand on the knee when travelling on public transport, I never had any problems with pedophiles as I was growing up, and neither, as far as I know, did John.

John Lennon:

We faced a similar potential risk of molestation when we wanted to see an A-rated film at the local cinema: the type of film where minors needed to be accompanied by an adult. We simply waited outside the cinema and, when an adult, usually a man, came up, we'd ask "Take us in mister?" If he agreed, we'd give him our ticket money, he'd take us in and we'd sit next to him.

It seems hard to credit nowadays, but Mimi didn't approve of John going to the cinema, unless it was to see a wholesome Walt Disney-style film. In her narrow view of what was and wasn't good for a growing boy, she regarded the cinema as a potentially corrupting influence, much as some parents now view television. But there was a lot that went on in the life of young John Lennon that Mimi didn't know about. John managed to get to the cinema under the pretence of doing other things. He became quite skilled at deceiving Mimi, who seemed to have little idea, at least until he was well into his teens, that her dear nephew was anything other than a well-mannered and well-behaved boy. The John Lennon his Aunt Mimi knew at home bore little resemblance to the John Lennon we all knew outside.

Hardly any homes had television. John's and mine certainly didn't. I remember we both saw TV together for the first time at Pete Shotton's house on a very early set his parents had just bought. It had a tiny twelve-inch screen in front of which a Perspex screen was fitted so as to enlarge the black and white image. We only stood there watching it for a few minutes out of curiosity and the novelty soon wore off. Whatever programme was showing wasn't designed to hold children's attention. I don't know about John, but I didn't see TV again until 1953, when I went to the next-door neighbour's house with my mother to sit for the whole day watching, on their new TV, the coronation of Queen Elizabeth The Second–the first time in the UK that TV had been broadcast for an entire day and evening.

In the absence of TV, the weekly children's matinee at the local cinema was a highlight of our young lives. Every Saturday morning, hordes of children descended like a swarm of locusts on the Plaza Cinema in Allerton Road. Inside the cinema, it was an absolute riot. We preferred to sit upstairs in the balcony. If we went in the stalls, we'd be sure to sit at the back of the cinema under the overhang of the balcony, as those in the front seats upstairs enjoyed raining their rubbish down on the heads of those exposed in the stalls below. We were able to yell and bounce up and down on the seats to our heart's content. Staff efforts to maintain quiet and order were futile and were soon abandoned.

The programme always included cartoons and westerns. The serials were a highlight, with the hero left at the end of each episode in some impossible situation from which he miraculously managed to escape at the start of the next week's episode. We loved these matinees and had great value for the sixpence it cost us to get in.

John Lennon:

The Plaza Cinema changed its name to the Gaumont in 1960, to the Odeon in 1962 and to the Classic in 1967. It closed its doors for the last time in 1971 when the building was demolished, being replaced by a new cinema in 1973.

Although few families had television, they all had a wireless and many people listened avidly to the BBC Light Programme, or to the more serious BBC Home Service. The highbrows listened to the BBC Third Programme. The chief censor at Mendips, Mimi, preferred this ultra-heavy station that John disrespectfully referred to out of her earshot as 'The Turd Programme'. Still, he was allowed to listen, as I did, to the daily quarter-hour serial on the Light Programme, *Dick Barton– Special Agent*, at 6.45 pm on weeknights.

With help from Uncle George, who rigged up an extension speaker in his bedroom, John was also able to hear some of the many good comedy shows, such as *Take It From Here* and *Life With The Lyons,* broadcast on the Light Programme. In my more enlightened home, as I got older, I was allowed to sit with the family on a weekend evening, in silence and with dimmed lights, and listen to a play on the wireless, much as families today sit together at home to watch a movie or a programme on TV.

The BBC had a monopoly of broadcasting in the UK and there were no commercial radio or TV stations. For those people who did have TV, there was only a single channel, with programmes broadcast only during the late afternoon and the evening in glorious black and white. These could only be watched on small screen receivers: no high definition, digital, LCD or plasma screen TVs in those days.

The only commercial radio station listened to in the UK was Radio Luxembourg, broadcast in English for several hours daily from the tiny country of that name in Europe. Lots of keen listeners tuned in to 208 metres on the medium wave band to hear this station. Although reception was sometimes poor, this was how, as a teenager, John Lennon would hear for the first time new songs from the likes of Elvis Presley.

Radio Luxembourg was important to us in our teenage years when we often tuned in to the weekly *Top Twenty Hit Parade*. This came on late in the evening after we were supposed to be asleep and, when we managed to stay awake, we listened to it in our bedrooms on a portable radio under the bedclothes. Earphones would have been useful. The station became a means of listening to hit parade records, as these were rarely played on the BBC stations. This was not due to simple bloody-mindedness on the part of the BBC, but was due to restrictions imposed on the broadcasting commission by the Musicians' Union, limiting the amount of recorded music that could be broadcast so as to create employment for musicians through the broadcast of live performances such as *Workers Playtime* and *Music While You Work*.

John Lennon:

So, the regular record playing sessions at my house, listening to Radio Luxembourg and to the few modern records at his mother's house, became the main sources of John Lennon's musical education between the ages of fourteen and sixteen.

Before this phase in our lives, though, children's programmes were popular with our pre-teens age group. Perhaps our favourite of these, when we were quite young, was the early Sunday evening Radio Luxembourg programme sponsored by the makers of the bedtime drink, Ovaltine. Throughout the UK, in cities and remote hamlets, countless young kids, including young John Lennon, would join in singing the jingle "We are the Ovaltinies, happy girls and boys…." There was a club to join and a badge to wear.

Another Radio Luxembourg programme popular with children was *The New Adventures of Dan Dare, Pilot of the Future,* serialised on weeknights at 7.15 pm. Then there was *Perry Mason* with its advertising message: "Brought to you by Tide. You get the world's cleanest wash when you turn to Tide." With no commercial radio or television in the UK, the advertisements on Radio Luxembourg were a novelty to listeners.

Chapter 9

Mucking Around

As boys growing up in the late 1940s and early 50s, and in contrast to today's TV and computer absorbed children, we spent a lot of our out of school time playing out of doors, often just mucking around and sometimes making mischief.

An enjoyable pastime for us at weekends, or during school holidays, was taking a trip on a double-decker corporation bus to downtown Liverpool. We always sat upstairs, in the front row seats, whenever possible. We usually got off the bus at the Pier Head terminus and, perhaps anticipating Gerry Marsden's famous 1964 hit song "Ferry Cross The Mersey", we caught the ferry to New Brighton, where we played on the beach and, if we had enough money, went to the funfair or to New Brighton Baths. Even in summer, the water in the big outdoor swimming pool was cold, but there were fountains, diving boards and slides to enjoy.

At the Pier Head, there was often a Punch and Judy Show—always good for a laugh. Sometimes, there was an old codger playing the spoons, maybe a juggler, sword swallower or fire-eater and, if we were lucky, an escape artist, all performing in the open air. The escapologists in particular fascinated us. In the best of these acts, a man was roped, chained, padlocked and rolled up in canvas. He had then to do the impossible and free himself. This he somehow always managed to do, and then, during the applause, his assistant passed the hat around. Most people threw some coins in. All this open-air street theatre in Liverpool, to which each of The Beatles was individually exposed, seems very likely to have influenced the style, years later, of The Beatles' films, video clips, cover art etc.

Quite apart from the free street theatre, the Pier Head had a lot to interest young boys. There was the floating landing stage where the busy river ferries were constantly coming and going. Then there was the floating roadway. Like the landing stage, this rose and fell by up to eleven metres (thirty three feet) with the huge tide. On the floating landing stage at the end of the floating roadway, you would often see one of the large and impressive white-painted Canadian Pacific passenger liners that ran between Liverpool and Eastern Canada. There were also the much smaller Isle of Man boats and the Irish ferries to Dublin and Belfast.

Out of school, I sometimes cycled over to Woolton to play with John and his Woolton friends. These invariably included Pete Shotton, usually Ivan Vaughan and Nigel Walley, and occasionally David Ashton. There was never any doubt it was John who was the undisputed leader of this little gang of boys.

The Boy Who Became a Legend

A regular pastime for us over there was sailing on homemade, and none too safe, rafts on Jackson's Pond, near Childwall Abbey Church, or on the pond at Foster's Field in Woolton. We used to catch frogspawn in season and tiny stickleback fish. Both were carried home in water-filled jars or tins by happy boys with muddy knees and clothes. How well I remember the distinctive stink of pond mud and the bright green pond slime.

On Vale Road behind John's house was the sandstone wall at the rear of an old strawberry-coloured Gothic house, the main entrance of which was on Beaconsfield Road, off Menlove Avenue. At the front of the house were large iron gates. Called Strawberry Field, it was originally a shipowner's mansion. At the time we played there, the Salvation Army was using it as a home for girls. The garden of the house was wild, overgrown and full of birds and rabbits. Once the wall had been climbed, it was an ideal place in which to play. John captured his fond memories of those carefree days in The Beatles' 1967 recording of "Strawberry Fields Forever", one of the most innovative and revolutionary recordings in pop music history.

The original mansion at Strawberry Field.

At other times, we'd frequently meet in the nearby Geoffrey Hughes Memorial Ground that we knew simply as the university playing fields. This extensive grassed area bordered Mather Avenue and extended to the back of Pitville Avenue and Pitville Road off Rose Lane in Mossley Hill. So for John and me it lay between our respective homes. This was another place where there was a deep pond, where we loved to swing far out over the water on a thick rope that someone years before had securely tied to a strong overhanging tree branch. This area was private property with 'No Trespassing' signs prominently displayed. This just added an element of danger to being there, in case we were spotted and chased off by someone in authority.

The Boy Who Became a Legend

On one memorable occasion, when I guess we would have been nine or ten years old, we were chased by a uniformed policeman all the way from the pond across the playing fields, with me in the lead trying not to stumble, John and the others following, and the policeman in hot pursuit, steadily gaining on us. You might well wonder why the police had nothing better to do than to chase little boys.

We were heading for the high metal fence that bordered the back of Pitville Road, thus away from John's house and in the direction of mine. "Don't trip up, whatever you do!" I yelled back to the others. "Follow me. I know a way out."

It seemed certain that the policeman would catch us with our backs to the metal railings of the high fence, but I knew something none of the others knew: there was one iron railing that had rusted through at the bottom and could be moved aside. This was the way I'd come in on my own several times. All I had to do was remember precisely where this particular railing was, make straight for it and get us safely through the fence before we were caught! With this railing pulled to one side, the gap was just wide enough for us to squeeze through but much too narrow for our adult pursuer to follow.

Fortunately, I found the right spot and led the others through. We made it in the nick of time. The high railings now separated us from the out of breath and irate policeman, and we delighted in making rude gestures at him as we ran off laughing. Then

John said "Good one Mike. But we'd better not come back here for a while."

At about the same age, we developed a passion for gambling with playing-cards. My older brother and I had enjoyed being included in occasional low-stakes family card-games at home, with parents, uncles and aunts, so I guess I passed my enthusiasm for this activity on to John and the others who'd had no such exposure. We often played cards sitting on the grass in the park opposite my house. Our usual games were Shoot Pontoon, Three-Card Brag and Newmarket. The stakes were pennies and halfpennies, a few threepenny bits and some silver. I used to get home after a game to find my palm stained brown from the copper coins that had been tightly held in my hot sweaty hand.

While we played, we had to keep an eye open for the police, as playing cards for money in a public place was an offence. I never understood why this was so as I couldn't see what harm it did. Anyway, because what we were doing was against the law, we played in the middle of a field, so we had ample warning of approaching authority, allowing us to immediately abort the game and flee. The moment a policeman was seen approaching, we all ran like hell in the opposite direction. This was after the boy with the quickest reflexes had scooped up as much of the stake money on the ground as he could and had stuffed it into his pockets. I always tried to be that boy!

The Boy Who Became a Legend

Reflecting on our childhood in the 1940s and 50s, I think in comparison with today's children, we were, from a young age, allowed a much greater degree of freedom to play outside the home. Provided you were home for meals and bedtime, you could pretty well come and go as you pleased. Normally you were expected to tell your parents where you were going, but it didn't necessarily mean that was where you actually went. Of course there were no mobile phones to help keep tabs on us.

We used to meet at each other's houses or in one of the parks. After dark, we tended to congregate under one of the neighbourhood street lamps. I don't recall any parents of my friends having cars at this time. We walked, cycled or travelled by bus or tram to get to wherever it was we wanted to go and we all had lights on our pushbikes.

On Sundays, until they managed to wriggle out of it, most children known to us were compelled by their parents to attend Sunday school, even if, as was most often the case, the parents were not themselves regular churchgoers. Having their kids safely out of the house on a Sunday afternoon gave the parents an opportunity for intimacy, or just a welcome bit of peace and quiet to snooze off the after-effects of their traditional large Sunday roast lunch.

I went to Mossley Hill Church Sunday School. This wasn't too much of an ordeal, but I'm sure I'd have had a lot more fun if I'd been at the same Sunday school as John. Unfortunately for me, this wasn't the case, as he attended the Sunday school held in St Peter's Parish Church Hall in Woolton, destined to become famous a decade later as the venue for the first meeting between John Lennon and Paul McCartney. John, like me, was brought up in the Anglican faith and we found the traditional and rather high-church services in both St. Peter's and Mossley Hill rather heavy going. The churches themselves were impressive, being built of local sandstone with Mossley Hill being much larger and by far the most imposing.

John stuck it out at his Sunday school for longer than I did at mine. For a while he was even in the church choir, together with Nigel Walley, David Ashton and, occasionally, Pete Shotton. David Ashton put on the internet some evocative recollections of those days concerning John Lennon. These include an incident during a Sunday service when David, instead of listening to the minister's boring sermon from the pulpit, was quietly reading his Boy Scout's Pocket Diary. This publication included the Boy Scout's Law. John, who was sitting next to David in the choir-stalls and could see what he was reading, took the book off him, produced a pen, and promptly changed the law 'A boy scout is thrifty' so it read 'A boy scout is fifty'. David showed John's alteration to the boys sitting near to them, who laughed out loud, distracting the minister and disrupting the service. This is a nice example of the subversive John Lennon in action.

David also recalled another example of John Lennon's creative mind when, as an aside during a choir practise and in reference to the then polluted state of Liverpool's River Mersey, he altered a Shakespearian quotation from *The Merchant of Venice*, 'The quality of mercy is not strained' to 'The quality of Mersey is not pure'. This landed David in trouble when he repeated it in class at his school and was ordered by way of punishment to write out the correct Shakespearian quotation a hundred times.

I still find it hard to visualise John Lennon as a choirboy in a cassock and a white surplice at divine service. He was nobody's idea of an angel! According to Pete Shotton, he and John finally had the unique distinction of being banned from St. Peter's Church altogether. They had already earned a reputation for being disruptive, and the final straw occurred during the annual Harvest Festival service when St. Peter's Church, just like Mossley Hill Church, filled the space in front of the altar with flowers, fruit and vegetables. This was the centuries-old traditional way of giving thanks to God for the abundance of the year's harvest. When the rector came to lead the service with the singing of the famous Harvest Festival hymn, "We Plough the Fields and Scatter (the Good Seed on the Land)", he found the carefully arranged display disturbed, and some of the fruit missing. Lennon and Shotton were easily identified as the culprits. They were both banished from the church, bringing John's choir singing to an ignominious end.

John Lennon:

John and I were in the wolf cubs too, and we both went on to the boy scouts for a time. As was the case with Sunday school, he went to the cub pack in Woolton while I went in Mossley Hill. My scout troop was the 2nd Allerton, based at Clearview in Rose Lane, just below Mossley Hill Church, whereas his was the 3rd Allerton that met, as cubs, in the same Woolton church hall as the Sunday school. As David Ashton recalled, "John turned up from time to time at cubs and later at scouts. He never attended regularly."

There was a monthly church parade, when our 2nd Allerton troop, comprising both scouts and cubs, marched in military style from our scout hut, then up Rose Lane hill to a Sunday morning service at Mossley Hill Church. Once a year, we in the 2nd Allerton troop were on show in the Lord Mayor's Parade, together with all the scout troops from surrounding districts. We were always very smartly turned out in our scout or cub uniforms. For the scouts, the uniform comprised bush hat, shorts, collared shirt and navy blue and white neckerchiefs. We marched proudly behind our own brass band, with bugles blaring and drums banging, including the huge bass drum in the rear of the troop, carried and played by one of the senior Queen's Scouts, with a real leopard skin draped across his chest. Impressive too was the adult troop leader at the front of the column, who regularly tossed his long silver mace high in the air and deftly caught it while never breaking step.

The Boy Who Became a Legend

Another abiding memory of my time as a wolf cub with the 2nd Allerton troop is of an open-air production by the scouts of the famous Rudyard Kipling story *Kim*. The tall, skinny, twelve-year-old boy scout who took the demanding lead role as Kim the Jungle Boy, his body covered with cocoa to look like an Anglo-Indian boy, wearing swimming trunks and clutching a long spear, was Derek Nimmo. He went on to become a very successful comic actor on stage and television, and later a theatrical producer, in the UK and overseas. What a lot of talent came out of our little corner of Liverpool! Derek attended Quarry Bank High School at the same time that John and I were there but as he was two or three years older than us, we didn't know him.

From the age of nine, John used to go off for weeks at a time during the long summer school holidays to stay with his Aunt Elizabeth (one of his mother's older sisters) in Edinburgh, travelling unaccompanied by bus. From Edinburgh he went with his relatives to their family cottage on the remote far north coast of Scotland. He always seemed to have a good time up there and on his return he regaled us with tales of adventures and misadventures in the wilds of Scotland. "Och aye the noo" he used to say to us. I never did understand what that meant but it sounded authentic! John looked back on his Scottish holidays as some of his happiest childhood memories.

Memorable family holidays for me during our four years at junior school included going a couple of times to the Isle of

Man. This took four and a half hours by ferry from Liverpool to Douglas, and for children the boat trip was an adventure in itself. We stayed in Ramsey, which had what seemed like endless wide flat sandy beaches, ideal for beach cricket and for swimming– not that we lingered long in the frigid waters of the Irish Sea. Oh, and we enjoyed seeing the unique Manx cats. Those are the ones with no tails.

Another time, when I was ten, I cycled with my parents and my older brother over sixty miles in one day from our home in Liverpool to Lake Bala in North Wales, where we stayed for a fortnight in a lakeside wooden cottage. This was a long bike ride for a ten-year-old and there I was pedaling away the whole day, at the same time that John was going on his holiday, reclining back in a bus. *Lazy sod, John Lennon*, I remember thinking. But, to be fair to John, at the end of our holiday we returned from North Wales to Liverpool by train.

Chapter 10

Lennon and Tarbuck

In the juniors at Dovedale Road School, John and I came to know another boy destined to become a famous entertainer, at least in the UK, and who was nearly a year older than us. This was Jimmy Tarbuck, who went on to become one of the best known and successful English comedians, and a celebrity golfer. He is also the father of high-profile actress and TV presenter in the UK, Liza Tarbuck. Jimmy lived near to Dovedale Road School and to me, in one of the really big posh houses in Queens Drive. I had to smile when I read in the UK *Daily Mail Weekend* of 29 January 2000 that Jimmy had come 'from the grim back streets of Liverpool'. Far from it! There was nothing grim or back street about where Jimmy lived, any more than there was about where John Lennon lived.

John and Jimmy Tarbuck (right).

Jimmy's father was a successful bookmaker and his mother had been a chorus girl. He was brought up as a much loved and indulged child. For example, when it came time for him to have a full-sized bicycle, his father agreed to pay for him to have an expensive one hand built at a specialist shop at the top of Smithdown Road. Mr. Tarbuck senior asked my older brother Peter, who was also a friend of Jimmy's, to accompany his son to the shop to ensure he bought wisely. The bike that was tailor-made for Jimmy had a light alloy frame and top-of-the-range Campagnolo gears.

Not long after this, John and I, at the age of eleven, were each given new bikes as a reward for passing the Eleven Plus examination to gain entry to grammar school. These were standard production line green Raleigh Lenton Sports models with 3-speed Sturmey Archer gears. While we were both thrilled to get these, they looked pretty ordinary compared with Jimmy Tarbuck's very up-market handmade bike.

Jimmy never seemed to be short of money, and often had things that older children coveted. He had his own set of golf clubs by the age of ten and in time he became an accomplished golfer. When he was a year older than that, he was given a less useful present of an air rifle. Imagine giving an irresponsible eleven-year-old an air rifle! Jimmy often came to my house where he delighted in firing the air rifle at people's backsides out in the back garden. Those pellets could really sting! Another favourite trick of his, on leaving your house, was to pick up a lump of earth in the front garden and hurl it at you as you stood at the open front door, so if you didn't close the door quickly enough, the soil would go all over the hall carpet.

Still, I must say it was hard not to like Jimmy Tarbuck. He had a great personality, a really cheeky sense of humour and, more often than not, a big smile on his face. In the same *Daily Mail Weekend* article, Jimmy recalled an incident in Dovedale Road School the day after he had played truant. The teacher said to him, "Tarbuck, you should have been here yesterday" to which, without batting an eyelid, Jimmy at once replied "Why? What happened?" This cheeky answer got him punished as the class fell about laughing. He loved to make people laugh even then.

In many ways Jimmy had a lot in common with John Lennon, but his wit was never as caustic as John's. Even though Jimmy was quite short in stature, he was strong and stocky. He never seemed to be afraid of anyone, no matter how big they were, and he knew how to use his fists. I thought him a lot tougher than John and he was always brim-full of confidence. John did his best to keep out of his way, and he wasn't alone in that.

When interviewed on *The Parkinson Show* on television in the UK in 2000, Jimmy related an anecdote about watching a John Lennon performance one playtime at Dovedale Road School some fifty years before. A large group of boys, me included, was intently watching John as he attached a condom to a tap in the school toilets and filled it with water until it stretched to a huge size. Then, like the Pied Piper, he led us all down the corridor to an open classroom window through which he hurled his water bomb. It crashed onto the corrugated iron roof of a bicycle shed and burst with a loud bang with water flying everywhere. Most of the boys had never seen a condom before and had only a hazy idea what its purpose was. The more enlightened ones did their best to explain to the others.

A highlight of our time at Dovedale Road occurred in the summer of 1951 when many of the older boys in the school, including John and me (both aged ten), Jimmy Tarbuck (aged eleven) and Ivan Vaughan (aged nine), were taken by a group of teachers led by Fred Bolt, a stern but popular teacher, on a holiday for a week in Port St Mary in the Isle of Man. For most of us, it was the first time we'd been on holiday without our family. We were accommodated in dormitories in Rushden School and slept on camp beds. Each night after lights out, the ghost stories, bawdy jokes and dirty songs began and some nights we got out our tuck-boxes and had a midnight feast. During these after-dark activities in our dormitory, Jimmy Tarbuck was the star performer, with an extensive repertoire of jokes and dirty ditties. It was on this holiday that he taught me, at the tender age of ten, some of the verses of the vulgar song *"Twas on the Good Ship Venus, by Christ You Should Have Seen Us"*. Thanks Jimmy for some very happy memories.

The Boy Who Became a Legend

In the lead-up to the holiday, our parents had been asked by the school not to let us set off with money in our pockets, but instead to allow sixpence per day for pocket money, and to send this to the teacher in advance of the trip, so it could be doled out to us daily during the holiday. This was to ensure the boys wouldn't run out of spending money after the first day or two. Despite this, when we arrived in the Isle of Man, we were amazed when Jimmy Tarbuck showed us several bank notes he'd been sent away with. As it turned out, he was to put them to good use.

After we'd been at the camp for a few days, it was discovered, at one of the regular late afternoon roll-calls that Jimmy Tarbuck was missing. After searches and enquiries failed to find him, his parents and the police were notified. We learned the next day that Jimmy had turned up safely at his family home in Liverpool. Apparently, he'd decided he'd had enough unwelcome discipline and wanted to go home. It transpired that Fred Bolt had ticked him off for being late for something or other and had told him that, as a punishment, he'd have to help with the washing-up. I could just picture Jimmy muttering under his breath one of his choice expressions such as "Bugger this for a game of soldiers". So, without telling anyone, Jimmy had quietly packed his things and somehow got himself from Port St Mary to Douglas, where he bought a ticket for the boat back to the Pier Head in Liverpool. After disembarking from the boat in Liverpool, he took a taxi home.

John Lennon:

I remember thinking at the time that it was a pretty enterprising thing for an eleven-year-old boy to have done. It was the first time ever that a boy had run away from the annual Dovedale Road School camp. John Lennon, on the other hand, surprised us all by behaving more or less impeccably throughout this school holiday. There is no record of him having got into any scrapes or having instigated any mischief at all– decidedly out of character!

Chapter 11

Last Days at Dovedale

It was later in 1951 that the headmaster at Dovedale Road Primary School, Mr. Evans, decided the noble art of boxing would be a good way to toughen up the older boys. Several pairs of bulky juvenile boxing gloves were acquired, and a temporary boxing ring was duly rigged up in the school hall. The boys were invited to put on these gloves, get into the ring for three minutes and knock the blazes out of their opponent. Naturally, the school tough kids, Lennon and Tarbuck, were among those boys who volunteered to have a go. After all, they had reputations to uphold. They weren't set against each other. Instead, it was decided John would be put into the ring to box against our mutual friend, Tim Holmes.

As Tim related to me: "John and I were about the same height and weight, so on the face of it, we were evenly matched. Once our bout started, I managed to keep out of his way for a lot of the time, poking out a tentative fist in a flurry now and again, hoping to hit him. I still wince when I think of the clout he suddenly gave me. A lucky jab caught me smack on the nose, bringing tears to my eyes, after which I couldn't see John other than in a complete blur. I couldn't wait to get out of the ring. I must have managed to hit him but nothing seemed to slow him down. He was certainly the winner on points. The experience turned me off boxing for life."

In our last year at Dovedale Road, it was announced that there would be a school production of Robert Louis Stevenson's *Treasure Island.* This was one of John Lennon's favourite books and he successfully auditioned, being given a leading role as Squire Trelawney. He performed with great confidence in this role, although he had hoped to secure the part of the one-legged two-faced ship's cook and erstwhile pirate, Long John Silver, who was his favourite character in the book. Here lies the origin of one of the names of the musical group that John formed just four years later at grammar school in 1956–the one that developed into The Beatles. Initially called The Quarry Men, John subsequently altered the name of the group to The Silver Beetles and later, with a subtle change of spelling, to The Silver Beatles. Finally the 'Silver' was dropped, leaving the name simply as The Beatles.

In the school production, Tim Holmes found himself in a curious role, playing the part of Long John Silver's parrot, called Captain Flint, after the infamous buccaneer of that name. Fortunately, Tim wasn't called upon to exactly follow the book's plot by sitting on Long John Silver's shoulder. Rather, and more practically, he had to hide in a huge wicker basket placed at the front of the stage. A big live green parrot in a large birdcage was placed on top of the basket. Aided by a script and a small torch, Tim had to cry out in a parrot-like voice at appropriate moments in the action "pieces of eight, pieces of eight, pieces of eight". The director had apparently decided it would be easier to train Tim than to train the parrot.

As already mentioned, John Lennon loved to play around with words, and he had a clever way of inventing malapropisms, whereby a word is replaced by another of similar sound, but different meaning. He often had us laughing at his amusing efforts. Long John Silver in 'Lennon-speak' became Large John Saliva, and the then famous strict tempo dance bandleader of the day, Victor Silvester, became Victor Sou'wester. A 'digestive biscuit' became a 'suggestive biscuit'. When a general election was announced, John came out with the choice malapropism 'There's going to be a general erection'. Another one I also remember John saying was 'Peace on earth and good wool to all men'.

He also constantly invented spoonerisms, a play on words in which corresponding consonants or vowels are switched so that, for example, he changed 'buttered crusts' to 'cruttered busts'.

John Lennon:

John loved the gobbledygook of the British comedian, Stanley Unwin, and the way he mangled the English language. In 'Unwinese', good became 'goodlilode', which John shortened to 'goodly'. This became one of our 'in' words and we used it frequently in talking among ourselves. Unwin would have found much of John's writing 'remarkibold'.

In 1952, at the age of eleven, as we approached the end of

Dovedale Junior School class of 1951-52. John Lennon is in the back row, 5th from the left. Bob Hayes is next to John, 6th from the left. The author is in the 2nd row from the back, the last boy standing at the right of the photo. Tim Holmes is in the 2nd row from the front, the last boy sitting at the right. Don Beattie is 6th from the left in the same row.

our time at junior school, we prepared to sit for the much dreaded Eleven Plus examination. This was a critical point in our education. Failure to pass this exam meant being sent to a so-called secondary modern or a technical school for four years with the expectation of finishing schooling at age fifteen, followed perhaps by a trade apprenticeship or an unskilled dead-end job. Success meant going on to a grammar school for at least five years until the age of sixteen, then sitting the Ordinary Level examinations for the General Certificate of Education (GCE). Success in these O Level exams gave entry into white-collar employment or into the sixth form for a further two or three years of schooling in preparation for the Advanced Level GCE exams, success in which gave the opportunity to go on to university.

John was told how important it was for him to pass this Eleven Plus exam. He later recalled: "I was told if you don't pass the Eleven Plus, you're finished for life. So that was the only exam I ever passed because I was terrified to fail." We both succeeded in jumping this hurdle, as did Bob Hayes, Don Beattie and other friends. We all selected Quarry Bank High School as our preferred grammar school, and fortunately were all granted our first choice. Jimmy Tarbuck was among those who failed the exam and he went on to Rose Lane Secondary Modern. We didn't see as much of him after that.

We left behind our friend Ivan Vaughan to complete another year at Dovedale Road School, as he was in the academic year below ours, due to being quite a bit younger than us. Interestingly, in the light of his later critical introduction of John Lennon to Paul McCartney, he was born on 18 June 1942–the same day as Paul. Ivan and Paul had never met before they both

John Lennon: started a year later in September 1953 at another grammar school, the Liverpool Institute in Liverpool city centre.

Dovedale Road School register showing the schools that John and others went on to in 1952.

At the Liverpool Institute, Ivan and Paul became friends. It is just as well they did so, as otherwise it is unlikely that John Lennon and Paul McCartney would ever have met. Significantly, it appears that it was Ivan's parents who made the decision that their son should go to the Liverpool Institute, rather than to Quarry Bank, where he wanted to go, as most of his friends were there. The reason for their decision was their desire to distance Ivan from what they perceived to be the bad influence of his old friend John Lennon! So perhaps it is Ivan's parents we ultimately have to thank for what subsequently became the highly successful and significant Lennon and McCartney song writing and musical partnership. In such subtle ways is the course of history changed.

It was on 10 July 1952 that we came to the end of our seven years of primary school education. We were poised to make the steep step up to grammar school. The Eleven Plus exam turned out to be a big divider, as boys we'd been at school with for many years headed off to different grammar or secondary modern schools. It would prove to be the end of a good many friendships, but the beginning of others.

John left Dovedale Road County Primary School with reasonable credentials and with much of the mayhem he had instigated in his earlier years forgotten or at least forgiven. As for me, in my last year I was a model of good behaviour (well almost), and was the head boy of Clive House. So, both John and I went out on something of a high note.

I also had the distinction of still being the tallest boy in the whole school. Luckily I stopped growing at age fifteen as otherwise I wouldn't have got through doors without ducking my head.

After the long summer school holidays in that year of 1952, we were to find ourselves, once again, on the very lowest rung of the ladder, at our much bigger, and somewhat intimidating, new grammar school. We hadn't been at the bottom of the heap since we were five years old. A rude shock awaited us!

Chapter 12

Grammar School

"Dad, were you really at school with John Lennon?", my pretty fifteen-year-old daughter, Carolyn, asked me, wide-eyed. It was 1987. We were on a short family visit to England from our home in Australia, and I was reminiscing with my mother at her flat in Liverpool about my childhood years. "Yes Carolyn", I replied. "Not only were we at school together for twelve years but, more significantly, it was largely thanks to me that John Lennon became a musician—at least that's what he told people after he became so famous through the success of The Beatles."

A few days later, having decided to show my two Australian-born children where I was educated, I made a brief return visit to Quarry Bank High School, my first since John and I left there thirty years before at the end of our schooldays, when we were both aged sixteen, going on seventeen. With Carolyn, and her twelve-year-old brother Martin, I called unannounced at the school one morning, reported to the school office, and introduced myself, and the children, to the headmaster's secretary. I explained I had joined the school in September 1952, along with the late John Lennon. "Oh well then, we'd better look that up", she said, and took down from a shelf, conveniently at hand, the school register for the 1950s.

The leather-bound, handwritten book sprang open at the relevant page, having obviously been opened at the same place countless times since John Lennon became the school's most famous old boy. My children, and particularly Carolyn, were amazed when they saw my name and personal details on the same page as John's, with only a few lines separating my entry from his in the register. Wow! So dad wasn't kidding when he told us he'd been at school with the legendary John Lennon.

John's life as a guitar-playing art student and small-time rock 'n' roll musician after he left Quarry Bank High School in July 1957, and his phenomenal rise, five years later, from relative obscurity to global renown as the leader of the amazingly successful Beatles, and as one of the four most popular entertainers in the world, have been well documented. His life prior to that hasn't.

As he was growing up, John always sensed that somehow he was different from other people, and he didn't feel comfortable on the normal path. As a teenager, he found no answer to the question he sometimes asked himself: 'Am I crazy or am I a genius?'

On 4 September 1952, as John joined his new grammar school, neither he nor the school had any idea what to expect of the other. His intelligence and inherent ability were evident to those of us who knew him well, but we didn't know, any more than he did, whether he was destined for a life of high achievement, or one of mediocrity. Unfortunately, the education system at the time wasn't designed to cater for children who didn't respond to the standard teaching methods. It tended to marginalise them. At no stage during John's years at the school, did any of the teaching staff, or the students, recognise in this boy someone who had the potential to go on to become more famous and successful than any other student in the history of the school. Least of all was there any conception that he would achieve this fame and success as a musician and songwriter.

When the four of us–John Lennon and his best mate from Woolton, Pete Shotton, and me, with my best friend from Dovedale Road School, Don Beattie–started our five years together at Quarry Bank, one of the first things we were required to do was learn the words of the school song.

The opening lines of the song were:

Quarrymen old before our birth
Straining each muscle and sinew

With scant regard for these inspiring words, we cruised through our years at Quarry Bank with very little straining of muscles and sinews in either an academic or a sporting sense. Still, the school song did have a lasting impact on Pete Shotton, as it inspired him four years later in 1956 to give what he thought was an apt name to John Lennon's embryonic skiffle and rock 'n' roll group–The Quarry Men–a name John liked and accepted. But Pete used two words for the name rather than one as in the school song. This was because, as he said in his book *John Lennon – In My Life,* he wrongly thought the first line of the school song was 'Quarry men strong before our birth'. Contrary to what many authors would have you believe, John's group was never called The Quarrymen. The name on the business cards they had printed, in advertisements and on the group's drum kit was The Quarry Men. The plaque on St. Peter's Church Hall in Woolton (where Lennon met McCartney), unveiled in 1997, refers correctly to The Quarry Men performing there on 6 July 1957.

When we arrived at Quarry Bank High School at the start of our first term in September 1952, aged almost twelve and feeling very self-conscious in our smart new school uniforms, what confronted us was an impressive school, steeped in tradition, with fine buildings and its teaching staff wearing long black academic gowns. It was vastly different from primary school with far more students, most of them older and bigger than us. "Christ", remarked John, as we gazed at the masses of boys milling around the school on our first day there, "we're going to have to fight our way up through all this lot".

The school, in Harthill Road, Allerton, next door to the girls' grammar school, Calder High School, and opposite Calderstones Park, was attractively situated on a high ridge with its playing fields sloping down to the Church of All Hallows,

Allerton. The church, like the main building of the school, and the walls surrounding them, was built of locally quarried sandstone. The whole area was heavily wooded, with the nearest high quality housing of this quiet and relatively affluent suburb situated some distance away from the school.

The impressive private mansion that became Quarry Bank High School.

private mansion house for a prosperous timber merchant. This was reflected in the high quality internal woodwork that included lots of wood panelling, as well as an imposing staircase in the main hall, with fine carved banisters. The house had been built adjacent to the site of an old quarry and this is what gave the school its name.

The large room utilised as the headmaster's study was lined with the finest types of wood, and had a large and impressive fireplace–not that you were really able to appreciate the decor when you were summoned there for punishment! The original grandiose gentlemen's billiards-room, off the main entrance of the mansion, had been converted to a science laboratory. The newer classroom extensions were of a more conventional brick construction, as were the separate school assembly hall and the gymnasium. A swimming pool was added to the school after we left.

From the time it was opened as a state school in 1922, Quarry Bank High School had been organised along the lines of a British public school. This was hardly surprising, as its first headmaster had been educated at England's most exclusive public school, Eton College. Contrary to what is implied by their name, public schools in England are not in fact public at all, but are private schools, usually with expensive school fees.

Changing places, from the top tier of primary school, to the bottom ranks of a usually much larger high school, is something with which most children have to cope. Despite having ended my primary schooling as the head boy of my house, and with high grades, I found the transition to the grammar school curriculum more difficult and unsettling than John. For the first time in our lives, we had to start learning foreign languages like Latin, that seemed pointless to me as it was a dead language that nobody spoke, and French, that I struggled with, not to mention General Science, Geometry and Trigonometry, at which I didn't start well.

It is tempting, but would be unfair and untrue, to heap the blame for my poor first year performance on the diverting but distracting classroom activities of Lennon and Shotton. In fact, as we started off in our new grammar school, John and I found ourselves, for the first time in our schooldays, placed in different classes. All first year boys at the school were put at random into one of three first year classes, 1B, 1F or 1R.

The school authorities at Quarry Bank would have benefitted from a sorting hat like the one at Harry Potter's Hogwarts School of Witchcraft and Wizardry, as if they had had any pre-knowledge of the true characters of Lennon and Shotton, there is no way they would have placed them in the same class. As it was, these partners in mischief and mayhem were delighted to find themselves put together in class 1R, while Don Beattie and I were put into class 1B. Only at the end of this first school year were boys graded, according to their first year academic performance, into one of the second-year classes, ranked 2A, 2B and 2C.

By finishing my first year in grammar school in the bottom third of my class, I found myself in September 1953 placed in the C stream in class 2C, along with my friend Don Beattie. John Lennon and Pete Shotton did somewhat better than us and they moved on to 2B, still together as if joined at the hip. As their school performance deteriorated, however, they were soon put down a grade, and we were all happily reunited in the C stream, where we stayed for the remainder of our time at Quarry Bank. I had to smile when I read in Alan Clayson's book, *John Lennon*, his description of John as 'a C stream hard case'. He was right about the C stream but, by Liverpool standards, we were none of us real hard cases, even though John liked to pretend he was one.

I used to finish each school year in the top five or six of our C grade class but managed to avoid being right at the top– except in my final year at the school–as that could have resulted in my being moved up a grade and away from my best friends. As for John and Pete, they rapidly descended all the way to the bottom of the C grade and there they remained. Had there been a D grade, they would no doubt have descended to the bottom of it too, but the bottom of C was as far as they were able to fall. As Pete Shotton amusingly said about what happened to him and John, "We started together in our first year at the top and gradually sank together into the sub-basement".

Apart from actual classroom lessons, all school activities at Quarry Bank, and most particularly sporting activities, were conducted in houses. In many public schools, a majority of the students are boarders and the houses are separate buildings where the boarders sleep. At Quarry Bank, there were no distinct buildings for each house, just classrooms in the school that were allocated for use by each of the houses. The school day usually started with a house meeting, but on at least one day a week the whole school gathered in the assembly hall where the headmaster presided over hymns, prayers and official school announcements. The day ended back in your houseroom with forty-five minutes of so-called prep, or preparation of homework, but on one afternoon each week there was obligatory sport. For most boys, this meant football (soccer) in the winter and cricket in summer.

As first year boys, we were known as Newts, and we spent our first school year in Bailey House. This was named after the first headmaster of the school, R. F. Bailey. Then, from the start of year two, we were all put into one of the main school houses: there were eight of these. The house you were allocated to depended mostly on where you lived, thus Don Beattie and I were put into Sefton House, while John and Pete went into Woolton House, along with Rod Davis and Eric Griffiths.

As sports were played in house teams, this meant Don and I could never be in the same sports teams as John and Pete, not that they ever played sports if there was any way it could be avoided. In his book, *John Lennon*, author Ray Coleman quoted from an interview he had about John with Eric Oldman, John's housemaster at Woolton house, who was also a chemistry teacher. As Mr. Oldman recalled, "on football afternoons,

Lennon would slope off and we wouldn't be able to find him. He seemed determined not to conform to the rules. But he had a wit and a humour and ability."

Cross-country running, held several times a year, was harder for recalcitrants to avoid. All students at the school were obliged to participate, and were expected to do their best to bring credit to their respective house. We didn't find this form of activity much fun, especially in wintertime, running through Calderstones Park, sometimes in snow and slush. John and Pete were particular slouches and, as such, were invariably among the last to finish. Prefects were on duty in the park in an effort to prevent runners from taking shortcuts, but on one memorable occasion John and Pete managed to elude them. Unfortunately for them, having hidden for a while, they misjudged where the main body of runners was and, thinking they had passed, they rejoined the run. To their horror, they discovered themselves to be the first runners home. Not surprisingly, they were disqualified, and the only award they received was a detention after school. The rest of us had a good laugh at their expense when we learned about this lark that had gone wrong.

John Lennon:

Author aged 15 in school uniform. Look at all that hair!

The wearing of school uniform was compulsory at Quarry Bank, both in school and during travel between home and school. Failure to wear the correct and complete school uniform was a punishable offence. Sometimes the school prefects stationed themselves behind one of the stone walls surrounding the school grounds in an effort to catch any boy walking or cycling who was incorrectly attired, such as not wearing a school cap. During our time at the school, the requirement to wear a school cap was relaxed for the older boys who particularly resented having to wear the type of headgear they associated with young schoolboys and wolf cubs.

Besides the cap, the uniform included grey shorts or long trousers, white shirt, grey pullover and a black tie with diagonal pairs of gold stripes. The house to which a boy belonged could be seen from a distinct house colour featured on the school cap. The regulation black school blazer had an impressive breast

The Boy Who Became a Legend

badge of red and gold with four scallop shells above a stag's head and the school motto in Latin, 'Ex hoc metallo virtutem'.

This is usually translated, incorrectly, as 'From this rough metal we forge virtue'. I can't recall too much virtue among my contemporaries, and in many cases their metal was still pretty rough, even after five years of dedicated forging by Quarry Bank's teaching staff.

The stern headmaster, Ernie Taylor, is in the centre of the 3rd row from the front. In the 3rd row from the back, John Lennon is 2nd from the left, Pete Shotton 3rd and the author 5th.

Chapter 13

Punishment

Discipline at Quarry Bank was maintained by a systematic punishment structure. Minor misdemeanours in or outside of the classroom were punished by a black mark that could be awarded by both masters and prefects. Two black marks in a week earned you a detention. The detentions were usually for an hour after school, spent either sitting in the detention room, writing out lines, or outside around the school grounds on some work detail, such as picking up litter or sweeping leaves. The worst detention assignment was pulling the very heavy metal roller over the school cricket pitch. This was bloody hard work and we used to joke about how the poor Egyptian slaves must have felt when they were building the pyramids. Fortunately our overseer, the school caretaker, Albert 'Yocker' Yoxall, didn't use a whip but would have delighted in doing so had he thought he could get away with it! John, Pete, Don and I often found ourselves on detention together and we had plenty of practise at activities such as these.

Serious offences, or repeat minor offences, resulted in corporal punishment in the form of a caning. Unlike at junior school, where caning was administered on the hand in front of the class, caning in grammar school was carried out in private, and with the cane applied not to the hand but to the buttocks. It was usually the housemaster who gave the canings and I well remember my first one from R. Lancelot Burrows (known as 'Porky' on account of his rotundity) who was the unsmiling housemaster of Bailey House. He was a thickset man with a strong right arm. Two or three strokes of the cane were usual for first offenders, progressing to a maximum of six. It was just as well for us that the days of 'fifty lashes' were long gone!

More serious misdemeanours were referred to the headmaster, who seemed to work on a standard 'six of the best' when he judged caning to be called for, which he almost invariably did. What was serious in terms of misdemeanours was of course a matter of opinion. On one occasion, when we were aged fifteen, the four of us were given a caning by the headmaster for smoking a cigarette behind one of the bicycle sheds in the school grounds, where we had been spotted, and reported, by a prefect. Smoking was regarded in those days as a heinous crime, so much so in fact that we were warned by the headmaster that any repetition of the offence would most likely result in our expulsion from the school.

When we started at Quarry Bank, the headmaster was Ernest Taylor, who was always referred to, behind his back, as Ernie. He was something of a forbidding figure and was feared by the boys, especially by most of the younger ones. He was a very tall man, with a full head of grey hair, and always wore his long black academic robe. This flowed out behind him as he strode rapidly and purposefully through the school corridors, scattering young and older students who were quick to get out of his path. He was a devout Methodist, a lay preacher, an ex-serviceman, and a strict disciplinarian, not renowned for having a sense of humour.

An appointment with Mr. Taylor for a dressing down, followed by a caning, wasn't something you would look forward to. We were at the not so tender mercy of Ernie Taylor for the first four of our five years at Quarry Bank. He certainly knew who John Lennon was. John was one of his most caned pupils, whose name featured prominently in the official school punishment book.

On one memorable occasion, Mr. Taylor caned John (the usual six strokes on the backside) after he was caught gambling with playing-cards at the edge of the main school sports field, when he was supposed to be watching a championship cricket match between Quarry Bank's first eleven and a visiting team from another school. This seems a serious punishment for a fairly innocuous lapse of good behaviour, but in the judgement of the headmaster, John and the others in the card-game had badly let down the school. I don't know where I was at the time this happened, but this was one card-game I missed. I know I definitely wasn't in the cricket team and in any case would have picked a less exposed place in which to play cards for money.

The Boy Who Became a Legend

The others involved in this card-game were Pete Shotton, Don Beattie and Bob Hayes. They were caught along with John, and given the same punishment as him. All four of them were ordered to report to the headmaster's study on the following Monday morning. Bob can vividly recall the experience to this day. "On Monday morning I was ready to take the beating from Ernie. I had put on a pair of swimming trunks, two pairs of underpants and my football shorts, all under the regulation grey school trousers. The caning didn't hurt a bit. Only my pride was dented." This was the only time the normally very well behaved Bob was ever caned at Quarry Bank. It only served to illustrate the risks involved in hanging out with John Lennon and potentially getting caught up in his misdemeanours.

For the last year we spent at grammar school, we had a welcome change when, in 1956, a new thirty-five-year-old headmaster was appointed. In a parody of Oscar Wilde's famous play, *The Importance of Being Earnest,* he was also called Ernest or, to give him his full name, William Ernest Pobjoy. Fortunately, apart from one of his Christian names, he had little in common with his predecessor, and was soon both liked and respected.

Mr. Pobjoy tried to see the potential in every boy, and he was to be of some help to John after most teachers had given up on him. He encouraged John's interest in art and music, and only caned him once, although he did suspend him and Pete Shotton from school for a while on account of their persistent misbehaviour. Suspension from the school was the final step before expulsion, but by then John and Pete's time at Quarry Bank had almost come to an end anyway.

We learned later that, four years after we left the school, Mr. Pobjoy, on his own initiative, abolished corporal punishment at Quarry Bank. This was some twenty-five years before corporal punishment was abolished by statute in all schools throughout England and Wales. Unfortunately, his farsighted reform came too late to be of any benefit to John and other miscreants at Quarry Bank in the 1950s!

Chapter 14

Classroom Clown

As we settled into our new school environment, there were some of us who already knew John Lennon from having attended primary school with him, or from living near him in Woolton. To other new boys, and to older boys and staff, he was an unknown quantity, but not for long. He soon drew attention to himself and became a notorious figure in the classroom and around the school. At Quarry Bank, John became more renowned than revered. As he said in 1968, "People wanted me to be loveable but I was never that. Even at school I was just Lennon."

In class, John invariably sat at one of the wooden desks at the back of the room alongside Pete Shotton. Once we all came together in the same C stream class, Don Beattie and I usually sat with the two of them at the back of the classroom. As John's eyesight was so weak, and as he hardly ever wore his glasses, sitting further back meant he often couldn't read what a teacher was writing on the blackboard. This didn't help him to follow the lessons and was a factor in his becoming bored and restless.

Sometimes the laughs we had at school were at the teacher's expense, like the bucket of water that John balanced on top of a classroom door that wetted a teacher as he entered the classroom, amid howls of laughter from the class. On occasions, things would go too far and the teacher would lose control of the class. The boys in our first year at Quarry Bank were quick to distinguish the teachers who could maintain order from those who couldn't. They were also quick to exploit any perceived human weakness, and were sometimes quite heartless in pushing the teacher to breaking point, and beyond.

I am ashamed now when I recall how some experienced and dedicated teachers were quite literally reduced to tears in front of a class by the merciless behaviour of the boys, as they vied with each other in humiliating them. Our first year boys behaved in this way towards two kindly teachers, both quite old and short in stature, F.J. Greaves, known as 'Oscar', who taught English, and A.G. Paris, known as 'Biddy', who taught maths.

It has to be said that among his classmates John Lennon was unfortunately one of the ringleaders in this type of teacher baiting, or classroom terrorism, and he caused 'Oscar' Greaves in particular a lot of grief. As John grew older, there were a number of other incidents at school, when he gave new or student teachers such a hard time that they had no alternative than to send him to the headmaster. But he always stopped short of an actual physical assault on a teacher that might have led to his expulsion from the school.

The Boy Who Became a Legend

Many boys at Quarry Bank came to fear his acerbic tongue. He certainly knew how to be cruel and to take advantage of anyone, student or teacher, who evidenced weakness. But he wasn't vindictive.

There were some classmates who resented the punishments that were meted out to the entire class after John failed to own up to one of his misdemeanours, but nobody was prepared to point the blame at him. He admitted that at primary school he used to own up to any wrongdoing and take his punishment but, when he got to grammar school, he decided he wasn't going to do this any longer.

Many of the teachers at Quarry Bank were characters in their own right. One such was Ted Sankey whose job it was, in our first year at the school, to attempt to teach us the rudiments of the French language. Apart from the label on the HP Sauce bottle that graced every British dining table, and which was written in English on one side of the bottle and French on the other, few if any of us had ever had any exposure to this mellifluous, but very foreign, language. It says a lot for this teacher's abilities that at the end of a year of his French lessons, I was so utterly confused by the mysteries of French grammar and pronunciation that I took advantage of an option that was made available, to switch from French to Spanish at which language, with a different teacher, I did much better.

John Lennon:

In his classes, Ted Sankey would typically set the boys some work to do from the textbook; put up the lid of his wooden desk, hide behind it and proceed to read a newspaper. We soon discovered that the paper he usually read was the *Reveille*. This was a popular tabloid paper that featured lots of photos of young and usually scantily clad women, and sensational stories of the latest, and mostly sex-related, scandals. But Ted was very good at sensing the beginning of restlessness in the class and, without appearing to be attentive, he would suddenly look up from his newspaper, put his head around the raised lid of his desk, and hurl a piece of chalk, usually with surprising accuracy, at the head of an offending boy.

Ted Sankey used to teach us in the old main building of the school, in a large room that would have been the ballroom of the original mansion. It had a high ceiling and there were now folding wooden partitions that divided it into two classrooms. These partitions had panels in them that could be opened up, and in which it was possible to secrete a boy. This is precisely what John Lennon did on one occasion, before the start of the lesson, and before the teacher and most of the other boys had arrived. He pushed a hapless boy into the narrow space and told him, "You'd better stay there and be quiet until I let you out–or else." Then he closed the panel.

The French lesson was well underway when the boy, who couldn't stand being cooped up in the dark and confined space inside the panel for a moment longer, suddenly started banging to be let out and was released into the classroom, to the amazement of the teacher, and of most of the other boys, who had turned up for the lesson after the boy had been hidden away and hadn't been aware he was inside the wall panel. "Stop messing about Simmons," said Ted Sankey to the boy, as he was released from his hiding place to be greeted by laughter from the class and especially from John Lennon. Fortunately, the boy was too dazed, or too afraid, to say how he came to be in the panel, and this was one of many misdemeanours for which John avoided punishment.

The teachers were sometimes able to see the humour in Lennon's classroom pranks, and laughed along with the class. But rigging the blackboards, so they collapsed when the teacher attempted to write on them, wasn't well received. One escapade of John's that ended well for a change, and which soon became part of the school folklore, occurred in the weekly Religious Education class conducted by the very tall and broad John McDermott.

As Pete Shotton recalled in his book *John Lennon – In My Life*, he and John had realised this master hardly read homework papers and often returned them to students uncorrected. The class had been set a homework assignment to write an account of St Paul's journey from Jerusalem to Damascus, during which he was converted to Christianity when he was hit by a flash of light from the sky, heard the voice of Jesus, and was temporarily blinded. In his homework book, John had irreverently written something like 'On the road to Damascus, a burning pie flew out of the sky, hit St Paul between the eyes and knocked him down. When he came to, he was blind forevermore.' This sacrilegious but hilarious effort came back from the teacher with a tick as usual.

Thus emboldened, John decided that, for a laugh, he and Pete should make a white dog-collar for everyone in the class so as to surprise the master by giving him a class full of clergymen. They duly made these by cutting up the shiny white cardboard from breakfast cereal packets. Everyone in the class agreed to fasten one of these homemade clerical collars around their neck; then they nervously awaited the arrival of John McDermott. To quote Pete Shotton:

'In the event, the master strode directly to his desk, snapped open his briefcase, pulled out some papers and began reading in a dull monotone. Several minutes passed before he finally glanced up from his lecture, whereupon his mouth dropped in mid-sentence and his face froze into an attitude of disbelief. And then he laughed...and laughed…and laughed, his enormous frame shaking. "That was terrific boys," he finally gasped. "What a prank." He enjoyed it so much that he made us keep the collars round our necks for the duration of his lesson.'

In his book, Pete also reminisced about later on helping John with ideas that formed the genesis of his extraordinary song composition, "I Am The Walrus" and he quoted from the *Dead*

The Boy Who Became a Legend

Dog's Eye nonsense verse, as he remembered it from school. Unfortunately, he remembered it wrongly. The correct version–the one that so much appealed to us in our early days at Quarry Bank was:

'Yellow-matter custard, green-snot pie,
All mixed together with a dead dog's eye.
Spread it on a butty–spread it on thick
And then wash it down with a cup of cold sick.'

In case readers who are not from the north of England may be wondering what on Earth a 'butty' is, it is a bread and butter sandwich, as for example in a 'jam butty'. In John's song composition, the line in question came out as *'Yellow-matter custard, dripping from a dead dog's eye.'*

As part of our wider cultural education, or to support our studies of classic works in English Literature, we were taken several times to the Philharmonic Hall, not for a concert, but for a film. This famous hall,

The Philharmonic Hall, Liverpool.

generally referred to as 'The Phil', was in Hope Street in downtown Liverpool. It made a welcome break from the school routine, and I remember we were all impressed by the classic black and white Gary Cooper western *High Noon,* that we saw with the school on one of these enjoyable outings to the Phil.

On another occasion, the seniors from various Liverpool grammar schools, who were all studying *Henry V* for the forthcoming GCE English Literature examination, were taken to the Phil to see Lawrence Olivier in the definitive 1944 film version of this Shakespeare play. As usual, John's group of friends, including me, were sitting near to him. A Donald Duck cartoon preceded the main feature and as soon as the celebrated duck made its first appearance, John startled us by loudly and clearly proclaiming for all in the concert hall to hear, "There he is. There's old King Henry." This got a big laugh including from the supervising teachers. *Nice one, John*, we thought.

Chapter 15

Art and Writing

John Lennon didn't start off as a full-time clown at Quarry Bank and, when he was motivated, he could, and did do, good work, especially in Art and English. When he was aged twelve and in class 1R in his first year at Quarry Bank, 'Porky' Burrows set the class a project to illustrate the poems they were studying in English Literature lessons. The teacher was so impressed with the work that John submitted for this project, set out neatly in an exercise book titled *My Anthology*, that he retained it to show future generations of students what could be achieved. Showing his creative side, John had painted ten pages of watercolour cartoons illustrating the lyrics of poems such as *The Walrus and The Carpenter* and *Agincourt.*

Lancelot–what a splendid name for an English Literature teacher–Burrows held on to this exercise book throughout the remainder of his teaching career and during his retirement. When, some five years after he left Quarry Bank, John Lennon suddenly became very famous as the founder and leader of The Beatles, Mr. Burrows realised he was holding something of John's that might become a collector's item. Eventually, on his death, the exercise book passed to his son. Having long recognised its potential commercial value, the son offered it for sale at a London rock 'n' roll memorabilia auction in 2006. To his delight and amazement, it sold for the staggering amount of £126,500 (GB Pounds). I still find it hard to understand how a teacher can claim ownership of work done by a student, especially when it later turns out to be worth a fortune. It appears that the old saying 'possession is nine-tenths of the law' is true.

John loved to doodle in class and often did this while he should have been listening to the teacher. He sometimes had the class in hysterics as one of his funny and recognisable caricatures of a teacher, or a few funny words of his on a scrap of paper, was furtively passed from one boy's hand to another around the class. Even the well-behaved boys in the class were keen to get a glimpse of the latest Lennon creation.

John was an excellent cartoonist and I have often thought he might have made a good living as one. With the wisdom of hindsight, I wish I'd held on to some of those scraps of paper: they would now be very valuable. Many of them were tossed aside or ended up on the classroom floor, but some were intercepted by the teachers and were often good enough to be passed around and laughed at by their fellow teachers during morning tea break in their staff room.

Sometimes, John brought in from home an exercise book filled with cartoons and humorous captions in the form of a pseudo-newspaper that he called *The Daily Howl*. What I've always remembered as one of the gems of his humour was a weather forecast in *The Daily Howl* that was a clever word-play on the days of the week: 'Tomorrow will be Muggy, followed by Tuggy, Weggy, Thurggy and Friggy'. At the time he produced this, I thought it was a classic, and I still do. Another classic was: 'Our late editor is dead, he died of death, which killed him'.

Although John Lennon and Pete Shotton were the best of friends, John took a perverse delight in getting Pete into trouble in the classroom, for example by making him laugh, often when he needed to be serious, such as when he was answering a question from a teacher. When John did something funny out of sight of the teacher, or slipped some funny words or a cartoon in front of him when he was trying to concentrate, Pete was often unable to control his laughter. Thus it was Pete who got into trouble, receiving a black mark for disrupting the class, even though there was nobody more disruptive of classroom activities than John. While Pete was being admonished, John just sat there doing his best to look angelic.

As we moved up through the school, the high jinks continued in the classroom. John Lennon's cartoons, surreptitiously passed around during lessons, were increasingly inspired by the work of the artist and cartoonist, Ronald Searle–the creator of the St Trinian's School characters, including the sadistic schoolgirls.

John Lennon:

As an early demonstration of his distorted sense of humour, and of his back to front approach to composition, John became fond of drawing blind dogs wearing dark glasses and leading people who were able to see. This was a pun on the way 'seeing-eye' dogs for the blind were often referred to as 'blind dogs', and the supporting charity as The Blind Dog's Association (instead of The Guide Dogs for the Blind Association), as if it were the dogs that were blind rather than the people.

John also had a propensity to make his cartoon figures more grotesque, by drawing them as cripples or dwarfs and by adding hunchbacks, huge warts and any other deformities that he could conceive of and draw. In this way, he was able to make certain bodily features into a form of sick humour among his followers.

At one point, he took to drawing his figures with huge elongated earlobes so that when we saw someone who actually did have big earlobes, it became a private joke between us. We took to looking closely at people's ears, and identified some quite amazing specimens of extended earlobes. Fortunately, the people were usually in blissful ignorance of why we were choking with barely suppressed laughter. Even the simple utterance by John of the single word 'earlobes' at a serious moment in class would be enough to break our concentration– this of course being his objective.

The Boy Who Became a Legend

The cruel edge to John's humour was also reflected in the popularity among us of what were referred to as 'cruelly jokes'. Sadly, memory of these has faded, but one I remember as being typical of the genre went like this:

Question: Mummy, mummy, may I help with the washing up?

Answer: No Johnny, you know how it rusts your hook.

This conjured up in your mind a picture of a small boy with one hand missing and replaced by a steel hook, just like the pirates in *Peter Pan* and other such stories. This joke was a special favourite of John's, and perhaps reminded him of his stage appearance in *Treasure Island* at primary school.

It was in our last term at Quarry Bank that, for the first time in his life, John Lennon had one of his compositions published. This was a poem *The Tale of Hermit Fred*. It was published under the identifier, 'J.W.L. Vc' (meaning John Winston Lennon-Form 5c) in the school magazine, *The Quarry*, Volume X Number 2 Easter 1957:

'The wandering hermit Fred am I
With candlestick and bun
I knit spaghetti apple pie
And crumbs do I have fun!.......
I peel the bagpipes for my wife
And cut all Negroes' hair,
As breathing is my very life

John Lennon:

And stop I do not dare.'

John was later to have two bestselling books of similar doggerel published by the prestigious UK publisher, Jonathan Cape, but that was after he had achieved fame through The Beatles. In the first of these books, *John Lennon – In His Own Write,* he reproduced some of the cartoons and nonsense writing that he used to produce at school, several of which had appeared in *The Daily Howl*.

Reading the book, it is easy to see how John featured the names of his childhood friends in the stories–Nigel Walley in the story *Good Dog Nigel*, Ivan Vaughan in *Treasure Ivan* (a pun on *Treasure Island*) and Eric Griffiths in *The Fat Growth on Eric Herble*. Another nonsense tale *Sad Michael* was named for me (I was the only Michael among John's friends), with the policeman in the accompanying cartoon clearly recognisable as Pete Shotton, who in fact went on to become a police constable after he finished school.

From The Quarry magazine.

Chapter 16

Running Wild in Wales

Ted Sankey, our first year French teacher, had inherited a large crumbling old mansion, Dolfriog Hall, in the heart of the Snowdonia National Park in North Wales, at which, on a private basis but with the school's permission, he offered a holiday for year one and two students during the school Easter break in 1953, to raise some money towards the upkeep of the place. Many of us, John included, took up this offer and we had a fantastic and memorable time. The house was set deep in hilly green countryside, standing in its own extensive grounds, amid thickets of rhododendrons. It was quite isolated with no other houses in sight.

Dolfriog Hall in North Wales.

The Boy Who Became a Legend

A couple of miles away was a tiny hamlet called Nantmor, and one and a half miles further on was the pretty riverside village of Beddgelert. This could be reached on foot by walking through an unlit tunnel under a mountain. It had been built to carry a narrow-gauge railway, long since fallen into disuse, used to serve the copper mines operating at that time in the surrounding hills.

There were few organised activities for us boys during our holiday. On most days we were supplied with a picnic lunch and a drink, turned out of the house by nine in the morning and simply instructed not to return before four in the afternoon. So we were left free to explore, and terrorise, the surrounding region.

The most exciting and risky thing that a number of us, including John, did on several occasions, was to explore some of the old abandoned copper mines that we discovered as we roamed around the area. We penetrated deep into some of the old mine tunnels, which had been dug horizontally into the hillsides, following the rails of the old narrow-gauge railway lines that had never been removed.

The tunnel entrances had been sealed many years before when the mines were closed, but not effectively enough to keep out a band of determined boys bent on adventure. Wearing shorts and plimsolls, and in pitch darkness, we walked or waded through water up to a couple of feet deep that had seeped into the mine, as we very carefully felt our way along a tunnel with the aid of small torches. When we re-emerged into the daylight, we discovered that our bare legs had been stained a yellowy brown by the copper-coloured water.

The farm walls in the area were all built by the traditional dry stone method, using cut pieces of local slate and without any bonding material. One day, a boy in our group discovered how easy it was to lift a slate off the top of a wall and to send it hurtling down the steep slope on the other side. Other boys enthusiastically joined in and before long a significant part of the wall had been demolished.

When we'd had enough of this diverting vandalism, we walked back to our old mansion and soon forgot all about our mindless demolition job. But the farmer who owned the wall discovered the damage and, after making enquiries in the district, soon worked out who were the most likely culprits and where they could be found. At Ted Sankey's house a day or two later, in the presence of the angry farmer and the local police constable, we had the riot act read to us, after which we were made to return to the scene of our crime, and there to spend hours climbing down to the bottom of the gully, retrieving the slates, and carrying them laboriously back up to the top, so the wall could be rebuilt.

Boys being boys are capable of being pretty rotten to each other, and John was one of several such boys who were active during the holiday in non-scheduled activities such as 'ball-blacking'. This involved some unfortunate boy being grabbed by a number of other boys and held struggling on the ground, while his pants and underpants were pulled down and his genitals were liberally smeared with black shoe polish.

John brought prior experience to this form of bullying, in addition to his less aggressive interest in the male sex organs in our games of ball tick, or tag, at primary school. David Ashton remembered John as a young boy inciting his little gang in Woolton to grab a well-spoken boy from a private school, who had invited himself into one of their soccer games, then to pull down his shorts and underpants and to plaster his genitalia with a fresh cowpat (cow-dung). Most of John's gang got into trouble for that escapade, after the boy ran home crying and his irate and vengeful mother complained bitterly to their parents about the incident.

The sweet shop in the Welsh village of Nantmor, run by a little old lady we all called Ma Parry, did an unusually brisk trade during our holiday; but its profits were severely diminished when so many boys crowded into the tiny shop that several little monsters, including our hero, didn't just shop-lift the odd bottle or two of soft drink, but stole it an entire crate at a time, the contents of which were quickly shared out. Boys really can be little buggers when given half a chance.

John Lennon:

Given what we got up to, the residents of the area must have been pretty relieved to see the backs of the Quarry Bank party. Suffice it to say, Ted Sankey never organised another such holiday.

Chapter 17

Being a Nuisance

During school holidays, John Lennon and his sidekick, Pete Shotton, would sometimes cycle down to my house looking for something to do. They knew my mother worked, and, that if they found me at home, they'd be sure of a warm welcome.

We never met at John's place, as he preferred to get away to a less regimented environment whenever he had the chance. Also his Aunt Mimi seemed invariably to be at home and was very choosy about who she would let into the house. She wasn't noted for being welcoming to children who called uninvited, especially if they seemed high-spirited or a bit scruffy. This ruled out most of John's friends, me included. I never got past the front door step. Neither, years later, did Paul McCartney, who is quoted by Hunter Davies in his book, *The Beatles*, as saying, "I don't know Mimi. I was just the little kid that hung around with John. We didn't get into her house."

One day during a school holiday, when we were aged around twelve and I happened to be at home alone, John and Pete turned up unexpectedly at my house on their pushbikes. They were at a loose end and were seeking amusement. So I suggested for a bit of fun we should phone the fire brigade from my home telephone and make a false alarm call. "Great, Mike" was John's reaction. "Let's do that. It should be good for a laugh."

So, I made the phone call to the emergency number and put on an act of being in a house that was on fire, before pretending to collapse from smoke inhalation, dropping the telephone receiver on the tiled floor of our entrance hall for greater effect. "Fuckin' hell Mike. That was fantastic" said John. He and Pete were impressed by my impromptu performance. So too, it turned out, were the fire brigade. Of course, I hadn't given them my address when I rang them, and the game was to see if they would be able to trace the call.

Very soon we heard the alarm of an approaching fire engine. After all, the fire brigade didn't have far to come. As the three of us peeped out through the front room curtains, we saw a fire engine stop on the other side of the road, several houses up from my house, and the firemen starting to knock on doors. They had evidently been able to trace the call to the area but not to the precise house. "We'd better piss off quick in case they find us here and work out it was us who called" said Pete.

So, deciding to flee the scene of the crime forthwith, rather than hide in the house, we surreptitiously left one by one and fled as fast as we dared, trying not to draw attention to ourselves. I didn't return home for several hours and there were no repercussions. At least we proved that phone calls to the emergency services worked. But we didn't ever try it a second time. So much for amusing Lennon and Shotton!

It was during our first year at Quarry Bank that, with the intention of impressing John, I introduced him to the unusual pastime of gate-lifting. I'd had experience of this form of social nuisance around Mossley Hill with other friends of mine, and it was quite something for me to be able to lead John astray in a type of mischief he hadn't previously known about. Usually he was the one who did the leading.

To enhance the thrill of gate-lifting, we decided it had to be done in broad daylight, thus greatly increasing the risk of being caught. We did it together several times in Calderstones Drive, a narrow street leading from Allerton Road up to the school. All the houses in the street had a front gate that opened up to a garden path leading to the front door of the house.

To start off the gate-lifting process, you had to select the type of small wooden or wrought iron front garden gate that could easily be lifted off its gateposts. You then lifted off the selected gate and carried it at least five to ten houses along the street, until you found another gate of the same size that could also be lifted off. After this, you swapped the two gates over. So two unfortunate families were amazed, and far from pleased, to discover that their front gate had gone and been replaced by a different one. We often wondered how long it would take them to figure out what had happened and to set things right. We didn't hang around to find out. How the people must have cursed the perpetrators of this mischief, but of course we thought it was great fun.

Our friend Bob Hayes still remembers being involved in another more serious form of public nuisance. This was known as wall tumbling–pushing over brick walls that had cracks in the mortar. Another game Bob remembers enjoying with Tim Holmes was window bumping–trying to cause the collapse of pyramid stacks of cans of food in window displays in shops in Penny Lane or Smithdown Road. The method they employed was to bump the outside of the plate glass window with a clenched fist. If successful, the collapse of the neatly stacked pile of cans on the other side of the glass was very satisfying to young boys although, if done too hard, the glass would crack. What bad lads they were!

Bob also recalls when John revealed his compassionate side. "One redeeming feature of John Lennon was when we were aged fourteen and I met him on the grand staircase in the entry hall at Quarry Bank, just after my father died in 1954. He said how sorry he was–a spark of humanity after all. And yet, some years later, after we had left school and I met him when he was playing with his group in the Civil Service Club in Liverpool, he cut me dead. Maybe he just didn't want to know anyone with a proper job!"

The Boy Who Became a Legend

One day during a school holiday, when he and Pete were at my house, John staged an episode that was an early example of his highly developed sense of the absurd. He dared Pete and me to join him in dressing up in whatever odd clothing combinations we could find in the house, and then to walk down the street. The idea was to dress absurdly, but to behave normally. The fun was to observe people's reactions, and particularly their efforts to behave as if they hadn't noticed anything.

So we searched my house for dress up items. Some of the best ones came from my mother's bedroom wardrobe. They included a fox fur wrap made from the pelt of a dead fox with the animal's small head, complete with artificial teeth, forming the centrepiece into which the tail fitted. This must have been the height of fashion when my mother first wore it in the 1920s. It had intrigued me as a young child when I had first seen it, and it absolutely fascinated John as he wrapped it around his neck with glee. I wish I could remember precisely what else he chose to wear but I know it was an eclectic assortment. I do clearly remember that part of my outfit comprised a soccer boot on one foot and a Wellington boot on the other. Perhaps John wore the other half of each pair.

Eccentrically garbed, we strolled nonchalantly along the pavement of Dovedale Road to the bus stop near Rose Lane, and quietly joined the queue for the number 80 bus, amid soberly dressed Mossley Hill residents whose reactions tested our ability to restrain our laughter. Just as John had predicted, the people in the bus queue, and those we passed in the street, studiously avoided meeting our eyes, but stole furtive glances as they tried to work out what was going on.

Looking back at the scrapes we got into, and the mischief we got up to, in and out of grammar school, I realise it was only rarely that I was ever alone with John. He was almost invariably in the company of Pete Shotton and it became the accepted thing that wherever there was one, there too would be the other. They were always referred to at school as Lennon and Shotton– never the other way around. Pete was John's straight man in the double act for all of John's five years at grammar school. For the following three years that he spent at the art college, it was to be Stuart Sutcliffe who would fill this role.

Chapter 18

Money

Money, the lack of it, the need for it, and potential ways of getting it–without actually doing anything to earn it–were never far from the young John Lennon's mind.

One of the ways of increasing the cash flow, so as to finance the purchase of cigarettes and other items judged to be necessities, was to siphon off some of the money we were given at home every Monday morning, before setting off for school, to pay for our school lunches for the week. The students at Quarry Bank were required by the school rules to stay in school at lunchtimes and eat in the school canteen, either the subsidised hot meal provided by the school, or the packed lunch they had brought from home. Most boys, or their parents on their behalf, chose the cooked meal option. They were expected to buy their lunch tickets for the week every Monday morning at school.

We discovered that there were boys who preferred to fill up on snack food now and again at the school's tuck-shop, as an alternative to eating a sit-down meal. Then there were other boys who liked to duck out of the school grounds at lunchtime on one or more days a week instead of eating lunch at school. As we have noted, this is what John got into the habit of doing when he spent many of his lunch breaks at my house, in the course of which he furthered his musical education and ultimately came to recognise and begin to fulfil his musical destiny.

Many of the boys who didn't want to eat in the canteen every day still felt compelled to buy their lunch tickets for the week on a Monday morning, so as to be able to give a truthful answer to their mothers when, on a Monday afternoon on their return from school, they were asked the predictable question: "Did you buy your lunch tickets today with the money I gave you?" Having answered the question truthfully, these boys didn't see anything wrong in later quietly selling any of their unwanted lunch tickets to us at half price. As we had no scruples about putting our weekly lunch ticket money to other uses, we were happy to buy some of these tickets.

We reckoned that buying cut-price school lunch tickets for us to use on those days when we decided to stay at school, perhaps because it was raining, was a pretty good deal; but one afternoon, while they were on detention together and engaged in tidying the school grounds, John and Pete stumbled upon an even better scam. They discovered a large pile of old unused lunch tickets in a school rubbish bin. They suddenly saw before them the prospect of becoming rich. For the next couple of weeks, they did very nicely by selling these old and free tickets at half price to a careful selection of boys, until the school officials noticed a drop-off in weekly lunch ticket sales and started to become suspicious.

As a countermeasure to suspected fraud, it was decided that a new ticket colour would be introduced for each week; the tickets would be carefully checked when the boys presented them in the canteen to ensure they were of the current week's colour, and tickets issued in prior weeks–and thus of a different colour–would not be accepted. As soon as they heard about this new procedure, John and Pete tried to redeem any tickets they had sold that hadn't yet been used by the buyers, but they didn't manage to redeem all of them.

In an incident that could easily have led to the discovery of John and Pete's guilt, which would most likely have resulted in their expulsion from the school, my friend Don Beattie was detected using an old and illicit ticket that he'd bought from John. Fortunately for John and Pete, Don had his wits about him and his interrogators accepted his lie that the old ticket was left over from a day some time before when he'd had a day off school. John and Pete were greatly relieved by this outcome but they realised the game was up and promptly decided to destroy their remaining stock of old tickets. The scam had earned them quite a useful sum of money before they were obliged to shut down the operation.

John Lennon:

When they were a bit older, John and Pete volunteered to run a stall at the annual school fete, held to raise money for worthy school projects. You may well be wondering why our lazy and uninterested heroes were suddenly demonstrating such a public-spirited attitude. The truth is they saw it as an opportunity to have some fun and at the same time to make some money for themselves.

At their stall people paid to throw steel darts at a series of excellent caricatures of the Quarry Bank teachers drawn by John. The stall proved to be very popular with other students and it raised a surprising amount of cash. In their devious way, our two lads surreptitiously held back quite a lot of the takings for themselves instead of handing all the cash over to the school. Notwithstanding this, at morning assembly in the school hall on the next school day after the fete, they were, to their amazement, singled out for special public praise when it was announced that their stall had raised more money for the school than any other at the fete. "Fuckin' hell, Pete" said John quietly–this was how he prefaced most remarks–"we should have taken a bigger rake-off."

Shortage of money assumed greater importance in our lives as we advanced into our teenage years. It was one thing to live on only pocket money from your parents at the age of say ten or twelve, but quite something else to have to depend on pocket money as the only source of income from the age of fourteen upwards.

The minimum age for part-time employment in the UK was fourteen and the moment I reached it, I got myself a part-time job as a newspaper delivery boy at a newsagent's shop up in nearby Allerton Road. My paper round involved working for an hour or so on my bike from Mondays through to Saturdays, starting at around five pm, delivering the late afternoon edition of the *Liverpool Echo* to what were mostly large houses bordering Calderstones Park. This proved to be a lucrative area for tips at Christmas time. I preferred the afternoon paper round after school to doing paper deliveries in the mornings before school, which would have necessitated getting out of bed very early, even on dark and cold winter mornings. Getting out of bed at all in winter was no small feat when you awoke in a cold house that lacked central heating. I continued to do my newspaper delivery round until I left school in July 1957, at the age of sixteen years and nine months, to start full-time work.

During the Christmas holidays in 1956, in my last year at school, I successfully applied for what proved to be a great job delivering parcels for the Post Office from a temporary depot that had been set up for that purpose in my suburb. All other employees were casual labour, some of them unemployed people assigned by the Labour Exchange. Few of them knew the area. They did their deliveries slowly and on foot. I used my bike and soon learned I could do my assigned deliveries, go home for an hour or so, then report back for more parcels and still be greeted by a comment such as "Hello. Didn't expect you back so soon…"

I read that Paul McCartney took a similar Post Office delivery job in his last year at Liverpool Institute School. I hope he did as well as I did for tips. We were delivering right up to lunchtime on Christmas Day itself. On the morning of that day, I was working from a delivery truck, ringing the front doorbells and handing over parcels that contained presents and, in at least one case, a Christmas turkey that had been sent by parcel post. People could hardly have been more pleased with these last minute deliveries if Father Christmas himself had made the deliveries in a reindeer driven sleigh led by Rudolph the Red-Nosed Reindeer. It was obvious that some of the people had already started getting into the Christmas spirit, and this probably accounted for the generous tips I received.

When I needed to raise extra cash for something special, such as a holiday, I used to do casual gardening jobs around the neighbourhood, weeding garden beds or cutting lawns or the privet hedges that bordered most of the gardens. I found it easy enough to get work by ringing the doorbells of houses with unkempt gardens.

The money I earned from my paper round plus my pocket money enabled me, from the age of fourteen, to start to build up a good record collection. Each week I bought one or two 78 rpm single records in their plain brown paper sleeves. They cost about six shillings and eight pence each (33p in today's UK money or US$0.95 at the exchange rate applicable in 1954).

In later years, when John and Pete fondly recalled the frequent record sessions they had enjoyed at my house, they seemed mystified by how I had assembled such an extensive record collection. Pete thought–and said so in his book–that I must have had a relative who worked on the transatlantic liners and who brought me the latest records from the United States. Years later, John too recalled that "everyone knew someone on the boats. We in Liverpool were the first kids in Britain to get chewing gum and hear rock 'n' roll records." I did in fact have a relative, an older cousin, who worked on the transatlantic liners (as a purser on the famous 'Queen Mary' to be precise), as many of us did in Liverpool, but he never brought me any records.

The truth in my case was a lot more mundane and there was really no mystery about where I got my records. I simply worked to get the money to buy them. Most of them were bought from our local neighbourhood music shop up in Allerton Road and the rest were bought in downtown Liverpool

Working to earn your own money to buy whatever it was that you wanted, without being beholden to anyone else, was a strategy that seemed to hold no appeal for John or Pete. I remember them during our schooldays as being perpetually skint. The only work you ever heard John talking about was his cutting the lawns at home in Menlove Avenue to earn his weekly pocket money from Aunt Mimi. Even this chore he did with the greatest reluctance and usually only after several pointed reminders.

The British journalist, Maureen Cleave, described John in 1966 in an *Evening Standard* newspaper article as being 'probably the laziest person in England'. In an interview with The Beatles' official biographer, Hunter Davies, in 1968, the producer of their hit records and albums, Sir George Martin, was quoted as saying 'John is lazy, unlike Paul'. This was the John Lennon I remembered so well. He openly admitted to having 'a talent for skiving'.

John thought it was a lot easier to steal money, or to cadge it from others, than to work for it. When we were at school, he used to boast to me quite unashamedly of stealing money regularly from his Aunt Mimi's purse. His mother's partner, Bobby Dykins, unwittingly provided him with another source of ready cash. Bobby worked in the city as a waiter at Liverpool's top hotel, the Adelphi, and regularly came home with a pocketful of coins he'd received as tips. These he dropped into a big tin that he kept on top of a cupboard in the kitchen. This treasure trove proved irresistible to John once he learned about it, and whenever he could do so unseen, he used to help himself to a handful of coins. He reasoned that if Bobby noticed the hoard going down, he would assume it was his mother's doing.

An accomplished shop-lifter around the Woolton district from a young age, John found shops run by little old ladies to be easy targets. Rod Davis recalls that, as a kid, John used to steal Dinky toys from a shop in Woolton run by a Mr. and Mrs. Grace, and in his teens he stole records from the record shop a few doors away run by an old lady. He was lucky never to have been caught and prosecuted. Demonstrating that old habits are hard to break, John was still shop-lifting at the age of nineteen and twenty, whenever the opportunity presented itself.

On his first overseas trip, travelling to Hamburg with The Beatles in August 1960, during the road journey from the Dutch car ferry port when the group stopped briefly in the town of Arnhem, John emerged from a music shop with a mouth organ he boasted of having just stolen. During the group's second sojourn in Hamburg, he was reportedly shop-lifting regularly. By any standard of measurement, John Lennon, both during and after his schooldays, was an incorrigible shop-lifter.

Chapter 19

Growing Up

Like so many boys, John Lennon and friends, including me, reached puberty with no preparation or advance education by our families or our school. So, when the process began, it came as a real surprise to us. Our infantile enjoyment of dirty ditties and dirty jokes, only hazily understood, hadn't prepared us for developing sexuality with the physical changes this entailed.

If the age of puberty is the age when a boy begins the change to manhood then, by his own account, John started growing to manhood at the tender and relatively young age of eleven. The process started for me at the same age, but we knew of other boys who were thirteen before it began for them.

It was at the age of thirteen, too late to give most boys advance warning of what changes to expect to occur in their bodies, that we received our first and only sex education. This formed part of a biology lesson in our General Science class at school, dealing with human reproduction. There, not unexpectedly, a few sniggers during the lesson from boys who reckoned they knew all about it already.

It wasn't long before John was bragging at school about his sexual exploits. Most of us were sceptical of his claims, regarding them either as entirely fictional or at least grossly exaggerated. Still, our John could tell a good story and he liked and knew how to hold the attention of an audience.

From the age of almost eight, when we began our four years in the boys' only junior school, and during our early years at grammar school, we had little exposure to, or interest in, the opposite sex. Our sexual feelings, as they developed, were expressed within an exclusively male environment and I guess we were fourteen, going on fifteen, by the time we began to concern ourselves with girls: about the same age that we started to develop an interest in music. It was then that we got into the habit of hanging out, on Sunday afternoons and during the long light summer evenings, in Calderstones Park, opposite the school, where teenage girls also congregated.

We lounged around for hours on a grassy bank overlooking the park's boating lake, smoking, laughing and eyeing-up the girls. The challenge was always to separate a single girl from the herd, after which quite a lot of necking and tentative fumbling took place, stretched out on the grass in the warm afternoon sunshine or the fading evening light. If you were persistent and lucky, this might lead to more advanced explorations of the mysteries and wonders of the female form, perhaps in the darkness of the back row of the cinema.

Of course we had our teenage fantasies. John was especially besotted with the French actress, and so-called sex kitten,

Brigitte Bardot, with her long blonde hair. He had a picture of her pinned to the ceiling of his bedroom directly above his bed. On my bedroom wall, at the head of my bed, I had a large colour pin-up of the blonde American film star, Kim Novak.

Sex magazines for men also excited our imagination. John became a regular supplier of these. We never knew where he got them from, but suspected he stole them from shops. If he had any of them at home, he must have kept them well hidden from his Aunt Mimi, but then we all reckoned we were good at hiding stuff we didn't want our families to find. These magazines were passed around surreptitiously at school, as if found by the teachers, or for that matter by the prefects, they were likely to be confiscated. When that happened, we suspected the magazines were just as avidly read in the staff room or the prefects' room as they had been in the classroom or around the school. Be that as it might, they were never returned.

Playing cards for money was something that continued to divert us throughout our grammar school days, and it was often part of the record-playing sessions that John enjoyed so much at my house. On other occasions, we still played out in the open air, much as we had done as nine and ten-year-olds, but as we got older, or when the weather was cold or wet, we more often played at my empty family house. Poker, Three-Card Brag, Shoot Pontoon (Twenty One) and Newmarket were our preferred games and many friends used to turn up for one of these sessions. Stakes were not usually very high, but in a long session it was possible to win a worthwhile amount.

We first tried cigarette smoking when we were still wearing short pants, but it didn't become a regular habit with us until we were about fifteen years old. That was when, on most school days, we got into the highly risky habit of furtively smoking one or two cigarettes, or 'ciggies' as we called them, behind the bicycle sheds during school hours or, in a more relaxed and safer environment, out of school and often at my empty house.

We could usually only afford to smoke the cheapest and smallest cigarettes, like Woodbines or Players Weights. These could be bought in packets of five, ten or twenty and, if you were really hard up, it was usually possible to buy one or two single cigarettes. The brands that we smoked were known as Virginia cigarettes, on account of their tobacco type. Once, when I was in a shop with John and he had enough money to buy a whole packet, he played with words, as he so much enjoyed doing, and asked, in a deliberately expressionless way, for "ten Vagina cigarettes please". The whole point of this was, of course, to gauge the reaction of the tobacconist. This time the man behind the counter appeared not to register the deliberate error and didn't bat an eyelid. This delighted John. "Stupid bastard", he muttered to himself as we walked out of the shop. Life was never boring when you were out with John.

John soon became a heavy smoker and he remained addicted throughout his life. As an adult, he usually smoked strong French Gitanes cigarettes, with their distinctive aroma. On top of this, his high income as a successful entertainer funded his regular use of other more expensive and illegal mind-altering substances from marijuana to LSD and heroin. Perhaps it was just as well that nothing stronger than tobacco was available to us in our vulnerable teenage years.

Smoking provided us with sufficient means of demonstrating our approaching adulthood and we made only a limited exploration of alcohol during our schooldays. We were usually able to get away with buying bottled beer when we could afford it. But, entering a pub for the first time to buy ourselves draught beer across the bar was something we didn't pluck up the

Draught and bottled beer all ready for a party at home. The beer barrels are on a stone slab in the small pantry room next to the kitchen at 69, Dovedale Road under which the author used to sleep as a baby as some protection against night-time bombing raids.

courage to do until we were sixteen and could hope that, when he was busy, the barman wouldn't notice we were well below the minimum legal drinking age of eighteen years.

For the parties we had from time to time at our homes–but never at John's home–in our mid to late teens, we were able to have one or two small barrels of draught beer delivered to the house. Wines and spirits were beyond our finances, and our interest, at the time but we used to get a bottle of gin to mix with orange or lime juice, some white wine and Babycham, all to help to get the girls swinging. At this stage of John's life there was little sign of the anger and the dangerously aggressive behaviour that later came to characterise his drinking. What was apparent early on, though, was that he could get drunk very easily. He seemed to have a low tolerance of alcohol.

At school, by the time we were aged fifteen, John, Pete, Don and I, with a few others, had begun a low-key rebellion against being compelled to wear regulation school uniform. We went to school wearing socks in vivid colours like lime-green, orange or red, to brighten up the mandatory black leather school shoes and charcoal grey trousers. Even tying the school tie in a double-sided Windsor knot was a small act of rebellion. Outside of school, we started wearing narrow black denim jeans, or at least I did. John even went to the lengths of getting his mother to take in a pair of his long school trousers to make them narrower and more 'with it'. He didn't have the nerve to let his Aunt Mimi see him wearing these so he used to go out of the front door of

Mendips dressed in a standard-issue pair of school uniform trousers, with the other pair rolled up in his schoolbag, then he would quickly duck into a neighbour's overgrown garden to change them, reversing the procedure as he returned home.

John's Aunt Mimi used to read the riot act to him if she thought his clothing in any way resembled that of the so-called Teddy Boys. These were the often hard-case youths who were becoming more common and more violent on Merseyside. These young men were able to buy from their wages the pseudo-Edwardian Teddy Boy outfits of long drape jackets of blue or black velvet with heavily padded shoulders, worn with a bootlace tie, narrow drainpipe trousers, socks in vivid colours and thick crepe-soled shoes. Boots or shoes with steel toecaps were preferred, so as to be able to do real damage when the opportunity came to 'put the boot in' by kicking an opponent when he was down on the ground.

To enhance the Teddy boy image that we were consciously cultivating, and to mirror Elvis Presley, we all changed our hairstyles dramatically in our last two years at school, growing our sideburns longer and our hair longer and thicker. The sides were swept around and shaped at the back of the head into a DA (Duck's Arse) shape while at the front the top was combed up. John later said: "I wasn't really a Ted, just a rocker. I was only pretending to be one".

The Boy Who Became a Legend

He achieved a very effective Teddy boy image while still technically complying with school uniform rules. The photo of the whole school, 562 students and staff, taken in 1957 when we were aged sixteen and in our final term at Quarry Bank, shows John as a nascent Teddy boy, slouched forward and with a menacing facial expression. As the photo of the huge group was being taken with a scanning camera, John made a sarcastic comment that had Don Beattie, standing at John's left, doubled up with laughter just as the shutter came down. I am standing on Don's other side, looking amused while still managing to look at the camera. Pete is standing at John's right-hand side and he also looks amused. In this revealing and historic photo John, typically for him, is just scowling at the camera.

John Lennon:

Section of the Quarry Bank whole school photo of May 1957. In the 3rd row from the back of the photo, Pete Shotton is 4th from the left, John Lennon 5th, Don Beattie (looking down) 6th and the author 7th.

Chapter 20

Scousers

Although the British class system was well established in the 1950s, it wasn't much in evidence at Quarry Bank. All boys seemed to be judged on their merits and there were no obvious class barriers. Having said that, as all the boys were drawn from the relatively affluent suburbs surrounding the school, there were only a few boys from what might have been regarded as poorer working class families.

This meant that the thick Liverpudlian accent, or Scouse dialect, was hardly heard in the school. Few of us had much of an accent although, like all northerners in England, we would have been readily identified as such by our pronunciation of words, like aunt as 'ant' rather than 'arnt', and castle as 'cassel' rather than 'carsell'.

In most middle class families–and in families with aspirations to be thought of as middle class–the nasal Liverpool accent with 'th' pronounced as 'd' (as for example in 'dis' for this and 'dem' for them), was positively discouraged by the parents, and particularly by the mothers. This was the case in my family, and it was definitely so in John Lennon's, where his Aunt Mimi came down hard on any signs of John starting to speak like people who she would have disparagingly referred to as common, or lower class. In light of this, it is ironic that Mimi's next-door neighbours in Menlove Avenue reportedly considered her and her husband to be working class people, and looked down on them accordingly.

There was something of a class divide in those days based on the type of housing in which you lived. Those who owned their own houses or privately rented them, tended to some extent to regard those who lived on estates of Council-owned rental houses as their social inferiors. This was partly due to the progressive slum clearances in which the inner-city back-to-back slum houses that had survived the wartime bombing were demolished, with their decidedly working class inhabitants being moved to Council estates away from the downtown area. Apart from John, all the other Beatles lived in Council estates and it is known that Paul's mother discouraged him from speaking 'like Council estate people', in other words from using the Scouse dialect, or speaking with a Liverpudlian accent.

The John Lennon I knew through twelve years of schooling, certainly didn't have a Liverpudlian accent, nor did he speak Scouse. In Ray Coleman's book, *John Lennon,* John's first wife, Cynthia Lennon, is quoted as saying that John, with his upbringing, never had a real Scouse accent.

It was thus with some surprise, when John started to achieve fame as a rock star, that I heard him talking on the radio and on

The Boy Who Became a Legend

TV, with a distinctly Liverpudlian accent. It became apparent that he had cultivated this as part of his tough guy image while performing with The Quarry Men in what were often rough and unsophisticated neighbourhoods of Liverpool–the type of places where anyone not speaking with a Liverpudlian accent would be regarded with hostility and risk being roughed up.

Some of the places where the group was booked to perform were in districts where police patrolling on foot never walked alone. They always patrolled in pairs, and usually accompanied by an Alsatian police dog. The theme song of the supporters of the famous Liverpool Football Club, "You'll Never Walk Alone", was more appropriate than most people realised.

When The Beatles began their meteoric rise to fame, John's Aunt Mimi berated him about his Liverpudlian accent and told him "You weren't brought up to be a Scouser", to which he replied in a nasal accent, "De fans expect me ter talk like dat, yer know."

Judged by their family circumstances when they were boys, John out of the four Beatles would have been at the top of the social scale. Paul McCartney would have been next and George Harrison and Ringo Starr would have been right down at the bottom. Both George and Ringo, with their natural Liverpudlian accents, would have been widely regarded as true Scousers, and would most likely have been referred to as scruffs by boys from what were generally thought of as more affluent neighbourhoods, such as Woolton and Mossley Hill.

Years later in 1980, one of the last recordings made by John before his untimely death was a demo made in his home at The Dakota of his solo performance of a sharply satirical song he had written titled "Serve Yourself". In it, he gave full vent to his irreverent sense of humour as he sang it in his thickest Liverpudlian accent. He even used authentic Liverpool slang by shortening 'lad' to 'la'.

When this home recording was posthumously released by his widow, Yoko Ono, in 1998, as part of *John Lennon Anthology*, a 4-CD box set of previously unreleased tracks, then as the last track on a CD titled *Wonsaponatime*, it offended some listeners. But I must confess that when I first heard it I laughed out loud. This was the John Lennon I remembered from our schooldays with a wit that was razor-sharp, outrageous and often very funny.

Chapter 21

Amsterdam

It was in our fourth year at Quarry Bank, during the Easter school holidays in April 1956 that, as fifteen-year-olds, Pete Shotton, Don Beattie and I, with other school friends, took part in a schools exchange programme and went to Amsterdam–an experience that was to prove immensely significant for John Lennon, even though he didn't make the trip himself. I wish I knew why he didn't accompany us, but I guess the school would have vetoed his participation, as by this time he had earned such a reputation for disruptive behaviour that the school authorities would have been averse to taking the risk of his misbehaving, and thereby disgracing the whole Liverpool school's party. Perhaps he just couldn't be bothered to make the effort to go, or Mimi either didn't agree to his going, or simply couldn't afford the expense. Be that as it may, Pete Shotton went anyway, although it was decidedly out of character for him to do anything significant without John.

The group comprised thirty boys and thirty girls from various grammar schools in Liverpool, and each of us was paired off with a Dutch child of the same sex, and with a family background judged to be compatible with ours. Our group travelled over to Amsterdam at Easter 1956 and we each lived for ten days there in the home of the Dutch child with whom we were paired. This was reversed at the start of the summer school holidays when the Dutch children came over to Liverpool. In our Quarry Bank group, none of the boys who put their names down for this trip had ever been out of the UK before, so we all had to obtain our first passports.

On the morning of our departure from Liverpool's Lime Street Station, after meeting the children and teachers from the other Liverpool schools, we travelled as a group by train all the way down, via London's Euston and Liverpool Street Stations, to Harwich in the south east of England. From there we took the ferry across the North Sea to the Hook of Holland thence, again by train, to Amsterdam.

As for our good friend John, whom we'd left behind in Liverpool, it was to be another four years before he made his first trip out of the UK, when he was aged nineteen. Interestingly enough, it was at the Hook of Holland that John too first set foot on foreign soil. This was on 17 August 1960, when he travelled with The Beatles in an old minibus to Hamburg to fulfil the first of an eventual five contracts to perform in that North German city.

John finally made it to Amsterdam eight years after us, when he flew over with The Beatles to give a concert on 5 June 1964.

The Boy Who Became a Legend

Life for all of us, but especially for John, had changed beyond imagining during those eight years between our first trip to Amsterdam in 1956 and his in 1964.

Amsterdam school exchange holiday April 1956. From the left: The author, Pete Shotton, Mike Rice, Philip Burnett (teacher) and Don Beattie.

On the school exchange holiday, I was lucky to be paired off with a Dutch boy, Ronald Overwater, with whom I got on well. He was an only child, a year older than me, and lived with his parents in an apartment in Ceintuurbaan, in the centre of Amsterdam. His father was an accountant. It was the first time in my life that I'd been in an apartment as distinct from a house and the first time I'd taken a shower rather than a bath.

I enjoyed trying different foods, including such local specialities as raw herring and kroketten (deep fried croquettes of potato and meat ragout covered in breadcrumbs) that you could buy hot from coin-operated wall-mounted machines–all very futuristic I thought in 1956. I also remember for the first time in my life eating Wiener schnitzel with sauté potatoes in a smart restaurant in Arnhem, as a guest of Ronald's parents, and thinking it was the best meal I'd ever eaten. I'd never even heard of veal before, let alone eaten it. I'm not sure if John would have reacted with the same enthusiasm as I did, had he been with us. He was not an adventurous eater.

Amsterdam today is world-renowned as a city of extreme toleration where 'anything goes' and it was, by British standards, already a very liberated place in 1956 when we first went there. As fifteen-year-olds, we thought it fantastic to be able to sit openly and legally in a bar or at a pavement café, enjoying a tall glass of one of the city's fine draught beers and smoking a cigarette. What made it even more enjoyable for us was that the only teacher from our school who travelled with us, Philip Burnett, our young and broadminded English Language and Literature teacher, didn't show the slightest objection to our drinking and smoking in public. He was one of the few teachers who John respected and indeed liked. To my mind, this made it all the more of a pity that John wasn't with us in Holland.

On our return to Liverpool and before we returned to school, we told John that he would have loved Amsterdam, what a fabulous time we'd all had there, and about the sights of the city and the Dutch countryside that we had seen. I particularly remember John being intrigued by our recounting of the Amsterdam streets where prostitutes sat in the front windows of the buildings, advertising their services and trying to entice customers to come in and sample what was on offer. Four years later he was to discover for himself something similar, but on a much bigger and rougher canvas, as he explored and experienced Hamburg's infamous Reeperbahn and St. Pauli red-light districts.

What I refrained from telling John, until he came to my house at lunchtime on our first day back at school, was that I also found music shops in Amsterdam that stocked a wide selection of records, some of which hadn't been released or even broadcast in the UK. It was in one of these shops that I found a real gem in Little Richard's newly released "Long Tall Sally". What a sound! Little did I imagine, as I carefully packed this record in my suitcase to take back with me to Liverpool, how it would prove, after my return to England, to be the catalyst that would forever change John Lennon's life; nor could I possibly imagine the impact this change in him would ultimately have on the pop music scene in the UK and worldwide. From little things, big things grow.

John had been listening and singing along to records at my place for well over a year, and for a little while at his mother's too, but up to this point, it hadn't been more than simply an enjoyable and relaxing pastime for him.

When he wrote his book in 1983, John's closest friend, Pete Shotton, showed the sharp recall he still had of John's momentous and life-changing experience at my house twenty-seven years before in April 1956 that set him on a career path to fame and fortune as a composer and performing artist. This is what Pete had to say:

'It was through Mike Hill we were first introduced to the great black rock 'n' roll singers, notably Little Richard. Don Beattie, John and I got into the habit of spending our lunch hours at Mike's house, listening intently to Little Richard as we devoured our fish and chips.

On these occasions, however, John and I tried to affect a blasé attitude. John was proud of his reputation as Quarry Bank's leading rock 'n' roll aficionado and found it somewhat galling that Mike Hill and not he had made such a major discovery. In addition, both of us were loath to admit that this caterwauling coloured boy was every bit as electrifying as 'our' Elvis. But John's resistance crumbled in the face of "Long Tall Sally".

Chapter 22

Musical Destiny

Unbeknown to the others with me in the back lounge room at my house that April day, I had brought back with me from Holland a new record I had bought there by an artist none of us had ever heard of before: a short, dynamic and gay black American singer by the name of Richard Wayne Penniman, better known by his stage name, Little Richard. The A-side of the record, "Long Tall Sally", was a song he had co-written about a transvestite (perhaps his own alter ego), and it became his greatest hit. The B-side was "Slippin' and Slidin'".

The record had been released in the USA by Specialty Records of Los Angeles in March 1956 and simultaneously released in Europe on the now defunct Belgian label, Ronnex Records. It was the Ronnex version of the record, with its bright yellow label, that I was delighted to discover and buy, within days of its release, from a record store in Amsterdam.

I learned about this record from the young salesman in the store who had been turned on by the new sound. ('Turned on': at the time, a hip new phrase!) He told me that it had not long been delivered to the store, and he had only just put it on display. He played it for me there and then. I thought it was so great, with its wild, raucous vocal sound and rasping saxophone arrangement. I just had to buy it. I remember thinking to myself: *wait until John Lennon hears this*. At the time I bought the record, "Long Tall Sally" was unknown in the UK, so I felt I had something very special to take back with me to Liverpool.

On that spring lunchtime at my house in April 1956, as soon as everyone had settled down with their hot fish and chips, I said to John and the others, "I've got an amazing new record I want you to listen to. I bought it from a record shop in Amsterdam and it's by an artist who I think is far better than Elvis Presley." This apparently outrageous assertion immediately got John's full attention, just as I had intended it to. By tacit agreement, he was the leader of our group; he had an opinion on most things and was often scathing in his criticisms. Hence, when it came to anything new, we tended to look to him to give a critical lead. So I was very keen to see how he would react to this extraordinary new record I had discovered with its never-before-heard sound.

Amid all this, and even as I slid the heavy 78 from its brown paper sleeve, I deliberately didn't tell John or my other two friends the name of the song or the artist. They all looked up at me expectantly as I slotted "Long Tall Sally" on the spindle of the radiogram's auto-change stacker, turned the volume control up high, and hit play. The Californian recording by the singer from Georgia blasted into that northern English lounge room.

The Boy Who Became a Legend

The impact of the record on John was immediate and profound. Intense, silent and in sheer disbelief, he gaped at Richard's harsh, shrieked singing style, the relentless, powerful backbeat, and the pulsating of the two saxophones from the five-man backing group. For the whole two minutes and five seconds of this 'in your face' rock 'n' roll recording, John just sat there, unsmiling, his mouth open and his face registering absolute amazement. He was mesmerized.

When the record abruptly ended, the silence was palpable. No one spoke. We all looked at John, keen for his reaction. But he said nothing. For once in his life he was at a loss for words. We were all struck by how unusual this was. It was Pete Shotton who at last broke the silence. "Fuckin' hell", he said, "that was bloody fantastic, Mike. Let's hear the other side, then." Thrilled by what was happening, I played the B-side, Little Richard's hollering version of "Slippin' and Slidin'" and this recording also made a big impression on John and the others.

It was John's being struck dumb on first hearing Little Richard, rather than anything he did say when he finally found his voice, that anchored the events of that lunchtime in the memory of the three of us who together experienced his reaction.

John Lennon:

"Long Tall Sally" wasn't by any means the first rock 'n' roll record that John had heard for the first time at my house.

The actual Ronnex record that turned John Lennon onto rock 'n' roll - Little Richard's "Long Tall Sally".

Among others, I had often played him the three records I had by Bill Haley and His Comets, "Crazy Man, Crazy", "Rock Around the Clock" and "See You Later Alligator" (they were released in April 1953, May 1954 and February 1956 respectively), and while he enjoyed listening to these, they didn't have a life-changing impact on him.

The Boy Who Became a Legend

He was far more impressed the first time he heard Elvis Presley's "Heartbreak Hotel", although I always suspected he was more attracted by the song's theme of loneliness than by the tune or the performance of its singer. John could relate to this theme all too well as, since the age of five, he had known exactly what it was like to feel alone, despite always having other boys in his wake. His pain stemmed from his solitude and sense of being different from most of the boys he knew who lived with a mother and father, and often with brothers and sisters. John, on the other hand, had lived for the past ten years with an aunt and uncle as an only child.

"Heartbreak Hotel" had been released in January 1956, and been the subject of an article in the influential paper, *New Musical Express*. John listened out for Presley's record on Radio Luxembourg, and soon heard it played. He was sufficiently motivated to go out and buy it, even though there was no record player at his home. He had to wait until he visited his mother, when he could carry it over to her house and listen to it on her little portable Dansette record player. I didn't buy this record, as I never liked it.

Back in my lounge room on that day in April 1956, John was so overwhelmed by the raw power of the singing and the music of Little Richard and his group, and was so infected by my enthusiasm for the record, that he suddenly knew what he wanted do with his life; he made up his mind there and then to become a rock 'n' roll musician himself.

This is what John had to say in reflecting on the origins of his decision to take up music as a way of life and on his eventual meteoric rise to fame and fortune:

"Little Richard was one of the all-time greats. The first time I heard him a friend of mine (Mike Hill) had been to Holland and brought back a 78 with 'Long Tall Sally' on one side and 'Slippin' and Slidin'' on the other. It blew our heads–we'd never heard anyone sing like that in our lives, and all those saxes playing like crazy. The most exciting thing about early Little Richard was when he screamed just before the solo; that was howling. It used to make your hair stand on end when he did that long, long scream into the solo. I still love Little Richard. That's the music that brought me from the provinces of England to the world. That's what made me what I am.

Rock 'n' roll was *real*–everything else was unreal. It was the only thing to get through to me out of all the things that were happening when I was fifteen. I had no idea about doing music as a way of life until rock 'n' roll hit me. That's the music that inspired me to play music".

Most of John Lennon's biographers cite Lonnie Donegan's "Rock Island Line" or Elvis Presley's "Heartbreak Hotel" as having kicked off his musical career. Perhaps this is because these two records were among the very few that he bought and played at his mother's house. But whatever this frequent assertion is based on, it is just one of the enduring John Lennon myths. Yes, it is true that John liked these two records, but they didn't motivate him to make any changes in his life.

Nor was it the first Elvis Presley film, *Love Me Tender* that ignited his passion for rock 'n' roll. By the time this film was released in November 1956, John was already well and truly hooked on rock 'n' roll and his life had been forever changed by first hearing Little Richard's "Long Tall Sally" at my house the previous April. When he saw the Elvis film, he had been playing the guitar for six months already and had formed his own group. In his musical tastes, he had come to prefer the raw rock 'n' roll of Little Richard to the smoother rock, and the soft ballads, of Elvis Presley.

It really is amazing that in writing a biography of the man who could be said to be *the* most influential songwriter and recording artist of the twentieth century, so many biographers fail to correctly identify the key turning point of their subject's life – the one that caused him to resolve to become a musician. But this is what really happened: after hearing Little Richard for the first time at 69, Dovedale Road in Liverpool in April 1956, our friend John Lennon, at the age of fifteen, was motivated to emulate his rock 'n' roll heroes. The hitherto lethargic and uninterested classroom clown was galvanised into action. Within weeks of this life-changing experience, he took his first decisive step on the road to fame and fortune and towards fulfilling his musical destiny. He acquired his first guitar. Now all he had to do was learn how to play it!

Chapter 23

The Quarry Men

With a conviction like that of St. Paul on the road to Damascus, John Lennon, after his conversion to rock 'n' roll, became a believer–in his own ability to procure and learn to play a guitar. Determinedly, he first approached his Aunt Mimi to buy him one, but wasn't surprised when his request was emphatically rejected. Undeterred and without telling Mimi, he then approached his mother for help. Julia had always encouraged him in anything musical. It was she who came up with the ten pounds it cost to buy him a very basic guitar ordered from a newspaper advertisement, and to have it delivered to her address, thus circumventing Mimi. She then proceeded to teach him the basics of playing, although she only knew how to teach him banjo chords, the way she had been taught to play by her father on the mother-of-pearl backed banjo he had from his sea-going days.

In fact, John was only one of thousands of boys throughout the UK who bought guitars in 1956. Most of them had been inspired by the sudden popularity of skiffle music although, being inspired by a hot rocker, Little Richard, John always had his sights firmly set on learning to play rock 'n' roll rather than skiffle or folk music.

In 1955, I had bought a record by the Lonnie Donegan Skiffle Group called "Rock Island Line" with "John Henry" on the B-side. These two US railroad songs had been recorded and issued a year before as part of a band album, when Lonnie Donegan was a guitar player with Chris Barber's Jazz Band, before he formed his own group. The two songs had only just been released as a single. This took a while to take off, but by January 1956 Donegan's "Rock Island Line" had climbed to number one in the British hit parade.

This hit record, and Lonnie Donegan's appearances on television and in theatres around the UK, created a teenage fad in 1956 and 57, by popularising a form of music known as skiffle. All over the country, would-be musicians, most of them teenage boys, were motivated to buy guitars, intent on learning to make their own music. They got together to form skiffle groups so as to have a go at this do-it-yourself type of music.

Skiffle music was not in fact new. It had its origins in the USA in the 1920s, when black plantation workers, keen to make music but having no money, improvised their own instruments from such things as old metal washboards and washtubs. In the UK version, the bass sound of the washtub was replaced by a plywood tea-chest, with a broom handle and a length of string. Although both the music form and the songs were old, the

John Lennon: 1950s UK version of skiffle sounded new to a generation of British boys.

Donegan made the music more exciting by speeding it up and injecting his own frantic singing style. Boys throughout the UK tried to learn chords on their new guitars and struggled to copy the words of records such as Lonnie Donegan's "Rock Island Line", "Cumberland Gap" and "Puttin' On the Style" by playing them over and over again. The song "Freight Train" was also much copied. The version I had was by Liz Winters with Bob Cort and his Skiffle Group, and I still have the record to this day. Popular too was "Midnight Special". Like most of these songs, this was a traditional US railroad song.

John enjoyed listening to "Rock Island Line" at my house so much that he went out and bought his own copy that he played at his mother's house. It was the first record he had ever bought, but it didn't inspire him to think of becoming a musician himself. It took a few more months and a more dynamic

John's copy of "Rock Island Line", which he sold to Rod Davis.

performer than Lonnie Donegan to do that. Having rapidly lost interest in skiffle music as he pursued his first love, rock 'n' roll, John sold this by then well-worn record to Rod Davis in 1957. Rod still proudly owns it and has placed it on display in the British Music Experience exhibition in the O2 Bubble in London.

By the summer of 1956, approaching the age of sixteen, John was intently practising at playing his new guitar. So too was our friend and classmate, Eric Griffiths. John and Eric went to a guitar teacher in Hunt's Cross but gave up after only two lessons, which was why Julia taught them banjo chords as all they needed was to be able to accompany simple songs rather than to be able to read music, which was the guitar teacher's method.

Rod Davis, another Quarry Bank boy, younger than us but in a higher academic grade, had acquired a second-hand banjo soon after John and Eric got their guitars. Rod was a serious student, and not a close friend of theirs or mine, although John had known him since they had attended Sunday school together ten years before.

These three budding musicians, who all lived in Woolton, and who were all in Woolton House at school, soon began to practise together and before long a decision was made to form The Quarry Men. Right from the start it was clear that, although John Lennon could hardly play the guitar, he wanted to lead the group, just as he insisted on leading everything in which he was involved. Also, unlike the others, he liked to sing, so he became the group's undisputed lead singer. As Rod Davis remembers; "John wasn't bad, but he wasn't really seen as either a good singer or a good musician. But when we started playing at people's parties, we found that John could hold an audience".

The attraction of skiffle music for British boys of the 1950s–very few girls took it up–was that it was an affordable way of forming a musical group. Relatively cheap guitars and banjos were available and the washboard and thimble and a plywood tea-chest for the bass cost very little. The expensive item, and the biggest obstacle to young people trying to put a group together, was the drum kit, plus a drummer to play it.

The attraction of skiffle for one British boy in particular, John Lennon, was that it offered a way to realise his newfound ambition of being a rock 'n' roll lead singer and musician in his own group–yes, now he had an ambition for the first time in his life. The initial steps he had to take were first to buy a guitar, second to learn to play it, and third to form a skiffle group. He reckoned it shouldn't be such a big step to move on later from skiffle to rock 'n' roll.

Whereas for Eric and Rod, playing skiffle and folk music was what they wanted to do, for John it was only ever the means to a more exciting musical end. Interestingly, by the time their friend and the first manager of the group, Nigel Walley, had business cards printed for the group, these advertised

'Skiffle, Rock 'n' Roll and Country Western', but the later version of the card promoted 'Rock 'n' Roll and Skiffle', with the change in the order and the composition being deliberate and significant.

A skiffle group demanded a washboard player and John roped in a fourth Woolton House boy, his closest friend Pete Shotton, for this easy role–one that would clearly become redundant in a rock 'n' roll group. Pete was never an enthusiastic musician, but the habit of doing whatever John wanted him to do was deeply ingrained.

Finding a tea-chest bass player proved to be more problematic and several people came and went in this role. In October 1956, during rehearsals on the stage of the Quarry Bank School assembly hall in preparation for the group to play in the intermission of a sixth form Quarry Bank/ Calder High School dance–their first public performance–I even had a go myself: the nearest I ever got to playing with The Beatles! John had asked me earlier to fill this role but at the time I was totally focussed on studying, and trying to make up for a lot of lost time as end of school exams approached, so I had turned the offer down.

The boys finally settled on Len Garry to play bass. Len wasn't at Quarry Bank, but attended the Liverpool Institute where he was friendly with one of John's oldest friends, Ivan Vaughan, through whom he learned of the opening in the new group for a bass player. Len knew a bit about John through living, like the others, in Woolton. (Were there any boys living in Woolton who didn't know about John Lennon?) Len would have preferred to be a lead singer in the group, but he was willing to take the role that was available.

The challenge of finding a drummer with a drum kit willing to play with the group was addressed by Eric. He brought along a friend of his, Colin Hanton, who was older than the others and not a grammar school boy. He was already in the workforce as an apprentice upholsterer. Colin owned his own drum kit and said he was willing to be the group's drummer. That was enough and he was in. By the end of 1956, the six-man group was complete and comprised two guitars, a banjo, washboard, tea-chest bass and drums.

Few skiffle groups survived for more than a year or two, made any impact or moved on beyond private party or church hall performances. The Quarry Men was one that did, although only one of the original members of the group, John Lennon, remained with the group for long. The last of the initial members to drop out was Colin Hanton, sometime in 1958. The group was then without a regular drummer until they set off on their first engagement in Hamburg in August 1960 with Pete Best in that role, as the up-and-coming Beatles, after four years of evolution from the obscure Quarry Men.

Chapter 24

Going Nowhere

In June 1955, at the age of fourteen and towards the end of his third year at Quarry Bank, John's already shaky equilibrium was given a very severe jolt by the sudden and unexpected death, at the young age of fifty-nine, of his Uncle George, with whom John had lived since he was aged five. For almost ten years, George had been a good, kind and gentle friend to John, and a comforting refuge from Mimi's not infrequent wrath. As John was growing up, George was the nearest he had to a real caring father. It was Uncle George who taught him to read, draw and paint in water-colours. Perhaps the fact that his Uncle George too had been expelled from school gave them a special bond.

John took his Uncle George's death very badly. Coming as it did on top of his effective rejection by both of his parents that he had experienced a decade earlier, it had quite a devastating effect on him. It was as if one more safety brake or mooring rope had been taken off his life. His already mediocre academic performance at school plummeted to new depths as he became even less motivated to do any serious study, and even less respectful of authority than he had been before.

John Lennon:

As they moved up in the grammar school in terms of age, while moving down in terms of academic performance and behaviour, John and Pete were increasingly missing for all or part of a day, as they played truant from school: sagging off was what we called it. From about the time that his Uncle George died, John began to see a lot more of his mother, Julia, who was usually at home during the day, and appeared not to mind at all if John and Pete called on her when they should have been in school.

There seems little doubt that Julia encouraged her son in his eccentric behaviour and encouraged and supported his interest in music. Sadly, she wouldn't live to see its full flowering. Had she done so, she would have been immensely proud of her son's achievements.

It was during John Lennon's fourth school year, 1955-56, that he absorbed himself more and more in his newfound interest in music, at my house and, to some extent, at his mother's too. Then in April 1956, after his Little Richard revelation at my house, to quote the words of Pete Shotton: "Everything else in his life–school, family, even his own writing and drawing–was rapidly eclipsed by his obsession with rock 'n' roll."

Utterly lacking in motivation to achieve academic success, yet now a man obsessed with rock 'n' roll music, his new guitar and his new group, John Lennon, in his fifth and final year at

The Boy Who Became a Legend

Quarry Bank, 1956-57, took even less interest than previously in school work and made no preparations for the forthcoming GCE (General Certificate of Education) exams that were supposed to be the focal point of five years of study. It was no great surprise to those who knew him that in June 1957, at the age of sixteen, he failed to pass a single school-leaving exam, even failing in what was thought to be his strongest subject, art. He was in good company in this dismal performance as the same zero result was achieved (if one can use that word) by both Pete Shotton and Don Beattie. Eric Griffiths did better, managing to obtain three GCE 'O' levels.

John's cartoon that appeared in The Quarry school magazine, Christmas 1956.

Just before taking his school leaving exams, and anticipating his failure to pass a single one, John had a drawing published in the Christmas 1956 edition of the school magazine, *The Quarry*. Also, his own school reports had for some time made dismal reading, with damning remarks such as 'hopeless', 'rather a clown in class', 'wasting other pupil's time' and 'certainly on the road to failure'. Don't you just love this last one!

After my return from Amsterdam, I too underwent a major change and became focussed–not on rock 'n' roll like John–but on trying to get a good GCE pass in a year's time so I could get started on a decent career. This I managed to do, after a catch-up year of hard study, and surprised a lot of people by passing in six 'O' level subjects. The other Quarry Bank boy in John's Quarry Men, Rod Davis, had already passed several 'O' levels a year before. As the others left school, he stayed on in the sixth form, became head boy of the school and won a scholarship to read modern languages at Trinity College, Cambridge–some contrast to John!

As for John, he still didn't have the faintest idea of what he wanted to do with his life after finishing his schooling, nor of how he was going to support himself and make his own way in the world. As he progressed through his teens, he had formed an idea, not so much of what he could see himself doing, but rather of what he couldn't see himself doing. Above all, he couldn't envisage himself doing what almost everyone else did, which was to work in a regular job or profession. The prospect of working from nine to five in an office, or of working regular hours in a factory or as a tradesman, was anathema to John.

The Boy Who Became a Legend

Because he lacked motivation, he liked nothing better than to do nothing at all and be thoroughly idle. Fortunately for him, he had the talent, and above all the luck, to succeed outside the conventional work ethic system. In fact, he never worked for wages in a normal job for more than a few days in his entire life. Once he became extraordinarily successful, he valued the independence that financial success brought him–the ability to continue to do his own thing–more than he valued the money itself.

With only an unformed idea of continuing to play music and of following his rock 'n' roll dreams; with no school leaving qualifications and no career ambitions or prospects, John Lennon, at the end of twelve years of schooling, faced a bleak and unpromising future. Under the education system in England at the time, after completing five years at grammar school, pupils with a sufficient number of ordinary level GCE passes had the choice of staying on at school for a further two years in the sixth form, or of leaving school to join the work force, which is what I elected to do. Those like John who failed their exams had no choice but to leave.

Given his aversion to any form of hard work, John was happy enough to change from one type of schooling to another by accepting a place in a three-year course at the Liverpool College of Art that Mr. Pobjoy, his headmaster at Quarry Bank, had somehow managed to obtain for him–no mean feat on behalf of a student who didn't even have an ordinary level GCE pass in art. Mr. Pobjoy had apparently been prodded into taking action on behalf of John by some sharp words from Aunt Mimi who had sought an interview with him once she became aware of her nephew's situation.

As an art student, John received a student grant that provided him with a modest income. He boasted to me when I bumped into him in town one day, soon after we'd both left school, "I get paid for doing sweet bugger-all". This really appealed to his lazy nature. The art college regime also left him with plenty of unstructured time in which to develop his musical skills.

John maintained the uninterested attitude of his grammar school years and didn't take the art college seriously. "I went because there didn't seem to be any hope for me in any other field," he said. "And it was about the only thing I could do, possibly. But I didn't do very well there either, because I'm lazy. I wanted to be a painter, but I'd never have made one. I had no career that would have done me any good lined up. I stayed on (at art college) because it was better than working."

It was just as well that John wasn't forced into the labour market at the age of sixteen, given his poor prospects of obtaining a worthwhile job. His employment prospects as a musician were little better at this time. He had no formal musical training and couldn't read music. He had taken very little interest in music until, at the age of fourteen, he first began to listen to and enjoy my records. Even when he took up playing the guitar at the age of fifteen, it was years before he could play well.

At this stage, there was no intimation of the phenomenally successful future that awaited him through words and music. To most observers he really had the appearance of a school leaver who was going nowhere–a real nowhere boy with every prospect of becoming a nowhere man.

Chapter 25

Quarry Bank Remembered

You might by now have the impression that Quarry Bank High School when we were there was some kind of riotous establishment akin to a male version of the fictional anarchic school for girls, St. Trinian's. On the contrary, the teaching and facilities were of a high standard, with every opportunity for a boy, even one with little or no financial or other support or encouragement from his family, to work his way through to university, if he had the determination and ability. The school provided us with ample opportunity for a first-class education. To the extent that John Lennon and some of his friends failed to take full advantage of this, the fault, and the loss, was theirs.

I am sure that John, Pete and Don would agree with me in saying that we never at any time wished to be at, or thought we'd be better off at, another school. Although much of the information the teachers tried hard to force into us went over our heads, we all got some benefit from our years at Quarry Bank, even though we, and especially John, fell so far short of the expected standard of effort and behaviour.

Despite the often-troublesome years spent by John at Quarry Bank, he retained some fond memories of the school for the rest of his life. On the rare occasions in his adult life when he felt like wearing a tie, it was his old Quarry Bank High School tie he most often selected to wear. He was photographed wearing it in Japan in 1977, in New York in 1979 at the party for his 39th and his and Yoko Ono's son Sean's 4th birthday, and again in New York in 1980 at the age of forty. He had clearly grown very fond of this reminder of his unpromising schooldays.

Most men aged forty would long since have lost or thrown away their old school tie (I know I did), and it is somewhat ironic that a man who was perhaps the most uninterested pupil in the history of his school should, so many years later, still be

The Quarry Bank School building, now Calderstones School.

nostalgically wearing the very same tie he so detested having to wear, as part of an official uniform, when he attended the school as a student.

John Lennon:

I was also amazed to read in David Bedford's impressive and informative book *Liddypool: Birthplace of The Beatles* that John Lennon slept at The Dakota in New York with a picture of Quarry Bank School above his bed.

Quarry Bank High School, as we knew it in the late 1950s, no longer exists. This is due to the radical changes that have occurred in the education regime of the UK, such as the abolition of the Eleven Plus examination and of the two-stream grammar and secondary modern state school system, plus the move to co-educational schools. After undergoing various changes, the adjacent boys' and girls' grammar schools, Quarry Bank and Calder, were merged into one large campus now known as Calderstones School, a specialist science college.

In a move that could never have been imagined by the boys and girls of the two very separate schools in the 1950s, when the schools were merged, several openings were made in the high sandstone wall that had always separated the boys and the girls' schools and kept one sex hidden from the other. There were no opportunities for mixing of the sexes in our days, at least up to the end of the fifth school year, which was as far as we went. When we were at school, we always believed the high wall had been built to keep the boys away from the girls, but I guess it was designed to work the other way around as well.

When I was in England again in 2003, I decided to look in on my old school for only the second time since I'd left there

The Boy Who Became a Legend

forty-six years before. I found the old main school building–the original mansion house–just as I remembered it in the 1950s, and on my brief 1987 visit I hadn't penetrated any further than the school office. As I looked around further in 2003, I could see there had been some impressive structural improvements at the school including new buildings, although, as a consequence, the playing fields had shrunk.

When I arrived at the school in the afternoon in a rented car, I was surprised by how difficult it was to find a space in which to park; there were cars everywhere. My visit to the school in the afternoon happened to coincide with the end of the school day, and the reason for the glut of cars in the narrow road outside soon became apparent. They were there to pick up students. This was virtually unheard of when we were at the school. In our day almost all boys

The author in front of Quarry Bank High School main building in 2003. While the building looked unchanged from when the author and John Lennon were students there almost fifty years earlier, the same could not be said of the author.

went to and from school by bike, walked or took public transport. Being dropped off and collected by car would have been regarded as the height of ostentation, and something best done out of sight of other students.

Although I knew that since John and I had left there in 1957, the school had gone co-educational, it still came as a shock to see girls as well as boys, wearing what appeared to be Quarry Bank uniform, pouring out of the main school gates. It was even more of a shock to see how many students, mostly girls, lit up a cigarette the moment they got outside. Such a sight would have amazed John! Smoking in or near the school in school uniform was almost a hanging offence when we were students, but I guess nowadays there are more serious drugs for the school to be concerned about.

From what I saw on my 2003 visit, the racial mix of the students at the school was vastly different from what it was during our schooldays. This brought home to me the dramatic cultural changes that have occurred in British society since we lived there in England in the 1950s, when the only diversity we encountered at school was one of religion, as there were quite a few Jewish boys. They only stood out because they were excused from attending religious education classes and morning prayers. There was certainly no discrimination as far as we were aware, but some of them may have thought otherwise.

The Boy Who Became a Legend

I sometimes wonder what John would have made of the radical changes to the school at which he largely wasted five years of educational opportunities in the 1950s. As it was, he never went back to visit his old school. Had he done so, I like to think he would have been impressed, although the present focus on science wouldn't have suited his artistic temperament. But he would have enjoyed having girls, and a variety of cultural backgrounds, at the school, no corporal punishment and somewhat less emphasis on sport, as well as what is perhaps a more flexible and enlightened approach now to education for all students, and not just the mainstream children who tick all the right boxes.

Chapter 26

Musical Families

There was nothing predestined about John Winston Lennon becoming a musician and even less about him becoming a highly successful one. Apart from playing the mouth organ as a child, he had taken no more than a passing interest in music of any sort.

But we have seen how, by his own admission, his first hearing of Little Richard's powerful rendition of "Long Tall Sally" in 1956 proved to be the tipping point for fifteen-year-old John Lennon–the moment he resolved to take up playing and writing music himself. Up until then, he had drifted through life. Now he had something he could get passionate about. And it rapidly eclipsed every other interest in his life.

Musical talent is often inherited and in this respect John did have something going for him. Both of his parents had some musical ability and experience, although neither of them were professional musicians.

Alf Lennon, John's seagoing father, who was Liverpool born of Irish parents, intermittently played the banjo and did impersonations of Louis Armstrong and Al Jolson at ship's concerts on the high seas. He often regretted not having followed his instinct to pursue a career in entertainment, rather than as a ship's steward.

Alf's inspiration was his own father who was also named John Lennon. Alf's father died when he was only a boy, so his famous grandson never met him. Jack Lennon, as Alf's father was more commonly known, performed as a black and white minstrel at the height of the popularity of music hall entertainment in the UK and North America. In the 1890s, he toured the United States with Andrew Robertson's Kentucky Minstrels. As a boy, Alf Lennon himself had worked for a while with a popular children's group known as Will Murray's Gang, until the Liverpool orphanage, from which he had run away, found him and hauled him back.

Julia Lennon, John's vivacious mother, learned to play the accordion, piano, ukulele and banjo. She was an extrovert who loved to give impromptu performances and liked nothing better than to sing and dance. In her home, her little record player was in frequent use. Her vivacity was in marked contrast to the more serious demeanour of her eldest sister, Mimi.

John and his future musical partner, Paul McCartney, had very different musical backgrounds. In February 1953, Paul, at the age of ten and at his father's urging, auditioned for the Liverpool Anglican Cathedral Choir. He failed the audition. Had he passed it and remained in the choir, his life would most likely have followed a very different course. The intensive rehearsal and performance schedule of this prestigious choir would have left him with little or no time or energy to learn to play the guitar, and to join John Lennon's Quarry Men as a fifteen-year-old in 1957. Before flunking the Cathedral audition, and for a while afterwards, Paul sang in the choir at St. Barnabas Church in Penny Lane, near the roundabout at Smithdown Road.

Paul grew up with a father, Jim McCartney–a cotton broker born in 1902–who was an enthusiastic amateur musician. As a young single man in the 1920s, Jim had played piano and sung for several years in his own ragtime band: the Jim Mac Band. He was still single, and still playing, well into the 1930s. He was thirty-eight years old by the time he got married in 1941 to Mary Mohin, a maternity nurse, aged thirty-one.

There was a radiogram in Paul's home where he and his younger brother, Michael, heard lots of records, both ancient and modern. There was also a family piano that got plenty of use. By way of contrast, John Lennon grew up in a quiet home, with no record player and no piano, where he heard music only occasionally through the radio programs of the very conservative BBC. As he said himself, "In our family, the radio was hardly ever on". By this he meant that the radio was only turned on very selectively, rarely for music and never for pop music. Family members were expected to read in silence.

The Boy Who Became a Legend

Mimi actively discouraged John from listening to the latest pop music. She tried to impress on her young nephew her own taste in popular songs from the war and pre-war years. These included songs such as "Ain't She Sweet", "Let Him Go, Let Him Tarry", "Mares Eat Oats and Does (Doe as in female deer) Eat Oats" and "In The Shade of the Old Apple Tree". John was taught the vulgar version of this last one by his Uncle George, and he loved to sing it when he was out of earshot of his omnipresent Aunt Mimi.

As for live music, when he was a young child, John enjoyed listening to the Salvation Army brass band when it played at the annual Strawberry Field fete near his home, but his aunt and uncle never took him to a concert and he never had even a single music lesson. To my knowledge, the only musical performance he ever went to was when we were seniors together at Quarry Bank High School. We were taken down town to the Philharmonic Hall, where the world-famous Liverpool Philharmonic Orchestra gave a concert for students from various grammar schools.

I remember enjoying this and being impressed by seeing and hearing, for the first time in my life, a full concert orchestra with so many different instruments, many new to me. However, I also distinctly remember sitting in the concert hall near to the uninterested John Lennon, who declared it all to be "a fuckin' waste of time". Our teacher's efforts at school to teach us to read music were no more successful with John than they were with me. At the time, neither of us had the slightest interest in what we were being taught.

When he was a young child, John had been given a toy accordion on which he managed to produce a few recognisable tunes. Later, like many boys of his generation, he had been given a harmonica, better known as a mouth organ, as a birthday present from his Uncle George. My older brother had one of these too that he learned to play quite well, but I must admit my efforts to produce anything musical on it were a complete failure. John persisted in his efforts to learn to play his mouth organ and did a lot better than I did.

At the age of ten, on one of his annual bus trips to Edinburgh for a holiday, staying with another aunt, the driver of the bus was so impressed by his playing of his mouth organ all the long way to Scotland, that he presented him with a much better one that somebody had left behind on the bus on a previous trip. This high quality harmonica lasted him until, as we know, he stole a new one from a shop in Holland, on his way to Hamburg with The Beatles in August 1960.

Interestingly, it was John's harmonica playing that later influenced the choice of The Beatles' first hit record, recorded in September 1962. The record producer, George Martin, said "I chose "Love Me Do" as the best of the bunch in the end. It was John's harmonica playing that gave it its appeal." One can't help

The Boy Who Became a Legend

wondering if it was the stolen harmonica that John played on this historic occasion of recording The Beatles first hit record!

Chapter 27

Musical Foundations

Looking back on the second half of the 1950s, I have often reflected how very fortunate all of us were to be in our mid-teens during the birth of rock 'n' roll. What a great time it was to be growing up. The whole pop music scene was dramatically changing, right before our very eyes and ears. Musically, it was an exciting time.

I took to the new music like a duck to water, and before John did. I had more of a lead-in to music than he did, so I was a bit more advanced in a musical appreciation sense. Having a brother, Peter, who was nearly four years older than me, had given me a head start on most of my friends, including John. Peter was a keen jazz fan, who started off his interest in music with early blues and traditional jazz and moved on quite quickly to big bands and modern jazz. I followed in his wake.

At home, from the age of twelve, and through my early teens, I was fed a steady diet of jazz. I especially enjoyed listening to Peter's long-playing (LP) record of the celebrated 1938 Benny Goodman Carnegie Hall jazz concert, with its incredible solos by Benny Goodman, Harry James, Johnny Hodges, Lionel Hampton and Gene Krupa. This was a record that I played more than once to the Jazz Appreciation Society that I founded in 1955 at Quarry Bank School, as an offshoot of the already well-established Musical Appreciation Society. John didn't become a member, as he never really developed a liking for jazz. This was despite the fact that, from traditional blues through rhythm and blues, rock 'n' roll and jazz shared the same roots in the Negro music of the American South.

It was in 1954, when I was aged thirteen, that my mother bought a state of the art Pye radiogram–a combined radio and gramophone–for our home in Dovedale Road. This proved to be a source of great pleasure, not just for the family, but for my friends too. It was bought before we started to rent our first television about a year later. I always reckoned that by buying a radiogram before a TV, we had our priorities right.

The radiogram was an attractive piece of furniture. It had a freestanding lacquered wooden cabinet about a metre wide, with a big lift-up lid that exposed the multi-band radio on the left hand side, and the auto-change turntable on the right. It played the heavy and brittle 78 rpm records with one stylus and, by turning over the head of the turntable arm, there was another stylus for playing the very much lighter and unbreakable 33 rpm LP and 45 rpm extended play records.

You could stack up to eight records at a time on the auto-change stacker of the turntable. The powerful speakers were concealed behind the mesh front of the cabinet and records could be played at high volume with only minimal distortion. It produced a great sound, with a particularly good bass, and it stimulated me to start my own record collection. I was the envy of my friends, especially John Lennon, who didn't have any kind of record player at his home. No wonder he became fond of coming to my place to listen to my records.

From the age of fourteen, in September 1954, I started to buy records on a regular basis, and my collection soon grew to include a good selection of traditional jazz by leading British bands, including the Humphrey Lyttleton Band from London and the Saints Jazz Band from Manchester. It is worth noting that the records by these two well-known bands were produced by the then almost unknown London based producer, George Martin, and were issued on what was, at the time, an obscure recording label, Parlophone. A few years later, this small recording label–a division of the large EMI Group–was given an enormous commercial boost by George Martin's farsighted signing up of a Liverpool group called The Beatles, after all the leading record labels of the day had turned them away. At the time, the group was virtually unknown outside of Merseyside and the city of Hamburg.

Other 78 rpm jazz records I bought included some by Chris Barber's Jazz Band, The Dutch Swing College Band, Pee Wee Hunt and his Orchestra, and Fats Waller. By 1956, I was into buying the jazz greats on LPs. These included *Duke Ellington at*

The Boy Who Became a Legend

Newport and the fabulous *Count Basie Swings and Joe Williams Sings*–my all-time favourite jazz LP to this day.

I was able to get John to listen to a few of the jazz records in my collection, but it was to take another twenty years, until he was living in New York in the 1970's, for him to finally come to any real appreciation of jazz music.

My eclectic record collection soon included quite a few of the straight ballad hits of the time by such artists as Frankie Laine, Guy Mitchell and Alma Cogan. She, surprisingly, was one of John's favourites. They later met and, by some accounts, had an affair–perhaps one of his many infidelities as the only married Beatle. All of these top twenty hits were on standard 78 rpm records.

The first LP I ever bought was a ten-inch 33 rpm record of a live London Palladium concert by Johnnie Ray, an American singer who became famous through his hit record "Cry" and his very convincing stage performances. He was often called 'The King of Cry' or 'The Prince of Wails'. His career took off like a rocket and just as quickly crashed to earth, at least in the US.

John loved to listen to all these singers at my house and they remained favourites of his throughout his life. But no, I didn't have a single record by another of his favourites, and a surprising one: Bing Crosby. John's mother has to be given full credit for the Bing Crosby influence on him, as the crooner was one of her favourites. One of John's early compositions and top

John Lennon: twenty hits, in collaboration with Paul McCartney, was "Please Please Me", which had its origins in Bing Crosby's "Please" that he often heard at his mother's house. As already observed, playing around with words had intrigued John since he was very young and he never forgot the opening lyrics of this Bing Crosby song, with its play on the words 'please' and 'pleas'.

I became a huge fan of the American country and western singer, Hank Williams. Favourite records I had by him included "Jambalaya", "Your Cheatin' Heart", "Honky Tonk Blues", "Settin' The Woods On Fire" and "Baby We're Really In Love". I played these and other Hank Williams numbers so often to John Lennon that he too became a fan of this highly talented and highly-strung country music singer/ songwriter. As the author Philip Norman observed in his monumental book, *John Lennon – The Life,* in reference to John's group, The Quarry Men, 'John would do the occasional country number, like Hank Williams' "Honky Tonk Blues". He had in fact been a fan of Williams–the prototype singer/ songwriter well before Presley came along'.

At our frequent lunchtime record playing sessions at my house, my enthusiasm for singing along with the performers so infected John Lennon that he overcame his inhibitions and joined in. We particularly enjoyed singing along to Lonnie Donegan records, trying to keep up with the singer's fast delivery. Another great sing-along record from which John learned all the words, by playing the record over and over again at my house, was "Caribbean" by Mitchell Torok and the Louisiana Hayride Band, on the London label. This is another record I still have. We both loved the sound of the acoustic guitars and the words of this song.

Yet another favourite of ours was the Liverpool sea shanty "Maggie May", about a Liverpool prostitute who plied her trade in Liverpool's infamous Lime Street red-light district back in the sailing ship days. This became an early favourite of The Quarry Men. There are many different sets of lyrics for this traditional song but I liked the version sung by Stan Kelly in a thick Liverpudlian accent, that I had on a 45 rpm extended play record. It began like this:

Now come on all you sailor lads and listen to my plea
And when you've heard it once you'll pity me
For I was a bloody fool in the port of Liverpool
The first time that I came home from sea

And the chorus contained some great lines, such as:

For you've cheated many a whaler, now you've started off on jailors

But you'll never roam down Lime Street anymore

Best of all for singing along to were the Hank Williams records. Like Hank Williams fans everywhere, we struggled to decipher the lyrics he was singing in songs such as "Jambalaya", with its Creole words and idiomatic language, and in "Settin'

The Woods On Fire". Some of the words were totally unintelligible to us but we thought the tunes, the accent and the rhythm were all great.

John, as an adult and a successful performer, treasured fond memories of the musical foundations of his life, for which he was much in my debt. John told an interviewer "I listened to country music. I started imitating Hank Williams when I was fifteen, before I could play the guitar. I used to go round to a friend's house, because he had the record player, and we sang all that Lonnie Donegan stuff and Hank Williams. He had all the records." All the listening and singing to which John referred in this interview was in the back lounge room of my house at 69, Dovedale Road in Liverpool. My singing never made me anything more than happy but look what John's singing did for him!

Chapter 28

Merseybeat

Besides the records, and listening to the top twenty hits on Radio Luxembourg, I started to go to live performances, mostly to listen to jazz. There had been a ban for years by the Musicians' Union that had prevented overseas musicians from performing in the UK. When this was finally lifted in 1955, it presaged tours by legendary US artists who until then had only been known through their records and, in some cases, through movies. One of the first and most famous of these was 'the king of jazz' himself, the legendary Louis Armstrong, who toured the UK with his All Stars and vocalist Velma Middleton in May 1956.

The Liverpool concert of Louis Armstrong's first ever UK tour was staged in the Liverpool Stadium. The stadium was primarily a venue for boxing, although we used to go there sometimes on a Friday evening to watch the weekly all-in wrestling. The wrestling was always a riot; especially the tag matches with four wrestlers competing but with only two allowed to be in the ring at any one time. Often all four ended up in the ring together and it wasn't unusual for the referee to be bodily thrown out of the ring by one of the wrestlers allowing a free-for-all battle to ensue. The Liverpool crowds loved to hate the dirty wrestlers, especially the dirtiest of them all, Jack Pye. Although the whole thing was probably rigged, it was great fun and the audience used to shout itself hoarse. The old ladies sitting nearest the ring were the most vocal, booing and cheering with gusto.

For the Louis Armstrong concert, a revolving stage had been erected in the centre of the stadium to cater for a very different form of entertainment. The concert tickets had been exorbitantly priced, with the consequence that many of the most expensive seats remained unsold, leaving rows of empty seats near the stage. My cheaper ticket had still cost me the high price for 1956 of one pound ten shillings, a lot for a fifteen-year-old to pay. The moment the concert started, I was one of many who made a sudden dash forwards to fill the more costly empty seats nearer the stage.

It was a fabulous performance by a group of real jazz stars and with a great female vocalist. Throughout the concert, there was Louis Armstrong with his big trademark grin, blowing up a storm on his trumpet, singing, sweating profusely and mopping his brow with big white handkerchiefs. The concert was one to be treasured, as none of the audience had ever imagined they would see and hear this living legend of jazz in the flesh.

It was around this time in 1956, that I, and several of my friends, decided it was time we learned ballroom dancing, as this was one of the best ways in Liverpool to meet and socialise with girls. We duly enrolled at Vernon Johnson School of Dancing off Allerton Road and managed to persuade John and Pete to join us in this endeavour. Unfortunately, they only came once, after which John announced that he loathed any form of dancing and wasn't going to any more lessons. Pete, true to form, was reluctant to do anything different from John, so that was the end of learning to dance for him too. The rest of us had several more lessons from which we learned to dance the quickstep and the waltz.

We soon started going to Saturday night dances, usually at the Rialto Ballroom in town. This was easy for us to get to by bus and had a good dance floor and good live dance bands. We also went several times in our local area to St Barnabas Church Hall–always referred to as 'Barny's. This was on the corner of Dovedale Road and Penny Lane, just up from Dovedale Road School. It is still there and is now known as Dovedale Towers. It had the distinction, late in 1957, of being the venue for one of the early public performances by The Quarry Men, led by art student John Winston Lennon and featuring a recent new member of the group, the Liverpool Institute schoolboy, Paul McCartney.

Jiving was just starting to come into vogue, but it was banned in some ballrooms where they tried to limit the dancers to strict tempo ballroom dancing. Other places tried to restrict jiving to the area directly in front of the band. Before very long, jazz and rock 'n' roll clubs would turn most young people in Liverpool off ballroom dancing and, sadly, some of the finest ballrooms ended up being converted into Bingo halls.

A memorable musical event in my life in Liverpool was on 16 January 1957 when, aged sixteen, I queued up on a cold and wet night to get into the new jazz club, The Cavern, opening that night in Mathew Street, a narrow street of five and six-storey Victorian era brick warehouses, off North John Street in the city. I was there early enough to become one of the six hundred people who crammed into the cellar club, as many more than that were turned away.

The locally well-known and popular Merseysippi Jazz band was one of three jazz bands playing on that historic first night. There was also a skiffle group performing, but it wasn't The Quarry Men. I remember trying hard to convince John to come with me to the opening night of The Cavern, but he said he wouldn't, as he didn't like jazz. Quite apart from that, there was the usual problem of money. He never seemed to have any. He didn't earn any and his pocket money went mostly on buying cigarettes. Perhaps this was why he rarely went into town in the evening.

In its early years, The Cavern was strictly a jazz club. None of us, and least of all John, could possibly have envisaged that within three or four years, jazz would be phased out at the club, and that an as yet unknown group called The Beatles, featuring John Lennon, would make The Cavern world-famous.

The first time John set foot in The Cavern was in July 1957, just as he was leaving school and six months after the club opened, when, through a connection of the group's acting manager, Nigel Walley, The Quarry Men appeared there several times as a skiffle group. They were without Paul McCartney who had agreed to join the group, but who hadn't yet done so as he was away from home at the time attending a Boy Scout camp.

The group played on The Cavern's tiny stage in the interval between jazz bands: skiffle was tolerated at the jazz club on the basis that it was initially an offshoot of jazz. John's passion for rock 'n' roll got them into trouble when, at his urging and against the instincts of the others, they played a couple of rock 'n' roll numbers. A terse instruction was sent to them by the club management to "Cut out the bloody rock". After this, it came as no surprise to them that The Quarry Men weren't invited to perform there again.

It wasn't until early in 1961, after the group returned in some disarray from their first hectic sojourn in Hamburg, and The Cavern had been converted, under new ownership, from a jazz club to a rock music club, that John Lennon played at that soon to be famous venue again–this time as the leader of The Beatles. On 21 February 1961, John, Paul McCartney, George Harrison and drummer Pete Best played the first of their many lunchtime sessions at the club and, on 21 March, their first evening performance, one of three groups to perform that night.

It was in November of that same year, 1961, that Brian Epstein, the manager of the family owned music store, NEMS, situated in the next street to Mathew Street where The Cavern was, made his first visit to the club one lunchtime to see for himself The Beatles group that so many of his record buying customers had been telling him about. It was a momentous visit and one that dramatically changed his fortunes as well as those of The Beatles, as he soon ended up managing them full-time. Before long, as John famously said to the rest of the group, they were on their way 'to the toppermost of the poppermost'.

Before The Cavern succumbed to the upsurge in popularity of rock 'n' roll music, it was a very successful jazz club. One of the stars to perform there soon after it opened in 1957 was the famous Negro blues singer and guitar player, Big Bill Broonzy, who was backed by the Merseysippi Jazz Band. That was another memorable evening at The Cavern, when I happily queued up for admission. I read later on that Big Bill Broonzy was an inspiration for George Harrison. Whether George was there that evening at the club, or whether he only ever heard Big Bill Broonzy on records I don't know, as he was only fourteen years of age when this legendary performer, who died the following year aged sixty-five, appeared at The Cavern.

The Boy Who Became a Legend

I was at The Cavern on numerous occasions when it was a jazz club and when visiting jazz bands, mostly from the south of England, such as Chris Barber, Humphrey Lyttleton and Acker Bilk were featured. The keen jazz fans used to sit, in the central one of the three vaults of the old brick cellar, on hard wooden chairs of the type used in schools or church halls. The music was so loud in the confined space with its low ceiling that you were quite literally deafened by the time you emerged into the fresh air. Dancers filled the two side vaults.

The old cellar had previously been used to store fruit and vegetables. In its new usage the walls used to run wet with sweat and condensation as the air conditioning, such as it was, couldn't cope with the heat produced by the number of people packed into the club, many of them jiving energetically. Bits of plaster used to flake off the low ceiling, and rain down on the patrons as they danced, or sat listening to the music. We used to call it 'Cavern dandruff'. And you could usually smell urine from the toilets and the disinfectant used in an attempt to keep the place hygienic. We jokingly used to refer to The Cavern as the NHS club, meaning not the National Health Service but noise, heat and sweat. The atmosphere was smoky, smelly and electric. I loved it.

The Cavern didn't have a liquor license, so at break times the musicians used to climb up the eighteen steps of the narrow staircase that was the only point of entry and exit of the club, and troop up the narrow street for a few beers at The Grapes.

John Lennon:

This was an old pub on the other side of Mathew Street, quite near The Cavern. It is still in business today and looks much the same as it did in the 1950s. Keen band followers like me would follow in the wake of the musicians. I always thought it was so much better to hear these famous bands at The Cavern, rather than on stage at the Liverpool Empire or Picton Hall, as in that way you got to sit very close to the musicians while they were performing and, if you were lucky or just quick on your feet, you could meet and have a beer with them in The Grapes.

The early success of The Cavern as a jazz club led to the opening of the Mardi Gras Jazz Club eight months later on 28 September 1957. It was a better place for dancing to the bands, but I preferred the atmosphere of The Cavern. The other good club, The Iron Door, didn't open until 1960.

The best of all jazz nights, at least for dancing, were the annual Arts Balls held in the Liverpool College of Art, known to us simply as the art school. These gave the patrons non-stop traditional jazz. The live music was hot, and so were the dancers. It was a case of 'bop till you drop'. I can remember so well emerging at the end of the evening from the basement cafeteria where these functions were held, with my shirt soaking wet with

The Boy Who Became a Legend

sweat and then sitting with it clammy on my back as I rode home on the bus.

I souvenired from one of those nights a very large charcoal drawing of Frankenstein, with a bolt through his neck, that had formed part of the decorations on the stairway. I kept it for years and used to tape it up on a wall of my house whenever we had a party I don't recall ever seeing John at any of these art school functions, even when he was a student there, but then students had to buy an entry ticket along with other patrons and he didn't like either jazz or dancing. I guess in any case he could well have been playing with his own group somewhere else, as the balls were always held on a Saturday evening. I reckon he missed out on some very good times, but he did make it to some good parties at my house.

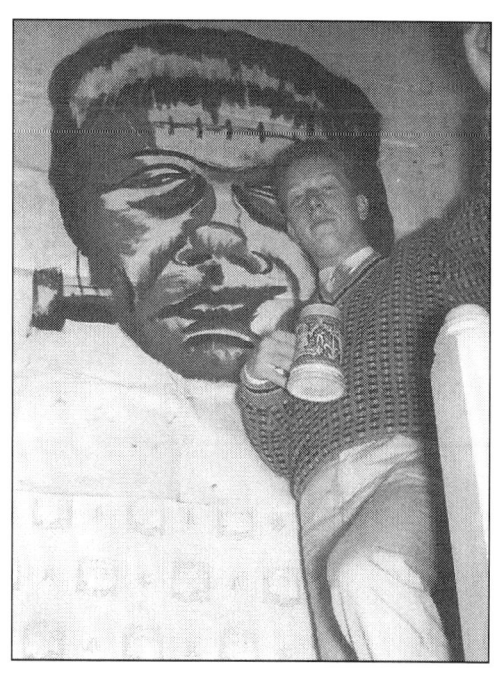

Frankenstein and the author at one of the parties at 69, Dovedale Road that John would have attended.

The Jacaranda Coffee Bar in Slater Street soon became another 'in place' in the city when it was opened in September

1958 by a stocky, black-bearded Welshman, Allan Williams, and his Chinese wife, Beryl. This was the year after I had left school and was immersing myself in the fascinating world of international marine insurance, of which Liverpool was then still an important centre. John meanwhile was doing as little as he could get away with at the art school. The Jac, as it soon became known, featured very attractive bright yellow striped pottery ashtrays in the shape of a Mexican sombrero. I made off with one just after the place opened and before they were all souvenired.

John recalled: "Everyone hung around in this club called the Jacaranda, which is near the art school in the centre of Liverpool. And we started hanging round there, before we really formed a band–when there was just me, Paul and George." This was when they were short of a drummer.

The Jac became a lively place, once the basement opened up and featured live bands. Allan Williams always joked, and with some truth, that he was 'the man who gave away The Beatles'. He certainly gave them a massive boost as a professional group by arranging their first contract to play in Hamburg's red-light district in August 1960, after they had played at the Jac a dozen times since the previous May. Although he was never appointed as the group's manager, he not only organised everything, but he personally escorted them to Hamburg by road and ferry in his own vehicle, to ensure they got there, safely and on time. This was after Allan, through promoter Larry Parnes, got them their first ever tour around Scotland in May 1960 as a still very raw group.

Liverpool's popular music scene was really coming alive from 1956 onwards, as local musicians and entrepreneurs laid the foundations for the sound that came to be known as Merseybeat. John was to be right in the thick of this but, like me, he was destined to soon leave Liverpool far behind, as he made his mark in the wider world. And what a mark it turned out to be!

Chapter 29

Anguish

As John first discerned, and then followed, the path to a musical future that opened up before him, how did he view the world as he grew into manhood? And what about his feelings for his family?

John had neither seen nor heard from his father since he parted from him in Blackpool when, as a five-year-old, he chose to remain with his mother on his parent's separation, never imagining that very soon he would find himself living and being raised by his Aunt Mimi. Throughout his schooldays, John carried within him the deep hurt and anger he felt about being, as he saw it, abandoned by his parents, first one and then the other, when he was only five years old, and about the memory of the traumatic times that preceded this.

His sense of victimisation was accentuated in 1955, when he was fourteen years old, by the totally unexpected and premature death of his de facto father, his dear Uncle George. After this bereavement, he began to see a lot more of his mother, Julia.

As John began, belatedly, to develop a more mature relationship with his mother, he soon formed a strong bond of affection and friendship with her. He was surprised and delighted to discover how much he and his mother actually had in common. She was fun to be with and they shared the same irreverent attitude to authority and a similar ability to laugh at the ridiculous. In stark contrast to his Aunt Mimi, his mother never chastised him, was never judgemental and was always supportive of his endeavours.

Tragically, John's increasingly rewarding relationship with his mother was brutally cut short when she was knocked down and killed by a car driven by an off-duty and unlicensed policeman outside Mimi's house on 15 July 1958, when John was aged seventeen and her daughters (John's half-sisters), Julia and Jackie, were aged eleven and eight respectively. At the time of this fatal accident, John was at his mother's house, where he had called on his way home, and was talking to Bobby Dykins while awaiting her return.

It was just a year since John had left school. His mother's sudden death left him utterly bereft. He was inconsolable and felt himself all the more intensely to be a victim of fate. As had been the case with him since the age of five, his grief and frustration manifested itself in angry and aggressive behaviour. But now he sought solace in drink. For a year or so he was more or less permanently drunk. This is how John reflected on this bleak period in his life:

John Lennon:

"It was the worst thing that ever happened to me. We'd caught up so much, Julia and me, in just a few years. We could communicate. We got on. She was great. I lost her twice. Once when I was moved in with my auntie. And once again at seventeen when she actually, physically died. That was very traumatic for me. That was really a hard thing for me. It made me very, very bitter. The underlying chip on my shoulder that I had got really bigger then. Being a teenager and a rock 'n' roller and an art student and my mother being killed, just when I was re-establishing a relationship with her. I was pretty self-destructive at college. I was a drunk and smashed phone boxes. It was mainly one long drinking session, but when you're eighteen or nineteen, you can put away a lot of drink and not hurt your body so much. I was in a blind rage for two years. I was either drunk or fighting."

Julia's death wasn't just a tragedy for John. It left his two young half-sisters without the caring mother they loved and needed and it left their father, Bobby Dykins, without the woman he had loved and lived with as his common-law wife for over twelve years. The consequences for all three of them were severe. Julia's strong-minded sisters, who had never accepted Julia's common-law husband or their two illegitimate children, had the girls made wards of court. None of the sisters, least of all Mimi, were willing to assume responsibility for rearing the girls but, after being shuffled around for many weeks without even being told their mother was dead, they went to live with the youngest of the sisters, Harriet, and her husband, Norman, at the small cottage in Woolton where John had lived for a while as a baby.

Due to never having married their mother, Bobby Dykins lost the custody of his own daughters, but paid maintenance and was allowed visiting rights. Sadly, less than eight years later, the girls lost their father too in yet another family tragedy when he died in Penny Lane early one morning in January 1966 after he crashed his car into a lamp post.

Shortly after his mother's death, a new girl, Cynthia Powell, started attending John's classes at the art college. They were soon dating and the relationship strengthened in 1959 when John moved out of his childhood home to share a student bedsitter with his new best friend, Stuart Sutcliffe, a fellow student at the art college and a very talented artist.

In 1962 at the age of twenty-one, John married Cynthia, after having made her pregnant. Their son, Julian, was born in April 1963. He was aged five when his parent's marriage broke up, and they were divorced in 1968. It is interesting to observe that, in a case of family history repeating itself, in the same way that John's father had spent hardly any time with John during the first five years of his life, John too spent very little time with Julian before he also effectively abandoned his son, when he married Yoko Ono and then moved to live in New York, never to return. The expression 'like father, like son' seems particularly apt.

Looking ahead to 1980, in another tragic family parallel, as seventeen-year-old Julian, who lived in England, was starting to develop a meaningful relationship with his father, who lived in New York–much as John had done with his absent mother in Liverpool–these growing bonds of affection and respect were brutally cut short by John's murder, just like they had been for John by his mother's accidental death, when he too was aged seventeen.

The other tragic parallel is the way four Lennon family sons through three generations all lost their fathers in various ways, before they reached the age of ten: John's father, Alf, by the death of his father; John himself, by the desertion of his father; John's first son, Julian, by his father's divorce and emigration to the US and his second son, Sean, by his father's murder.

So what about John's long missing father? In 1964, after he became aware, through media coverage, of his son's fame and fortune, Alf Lennon arranged to meet John to give him his side of the story of his separation from Julia, in an effort to counter Mimi's distorted version that had shown the fault to be entirely his. Not surprisingly perhaps, John gave his father a cool reception and it wasn't until 1967 that he and Alf were somewhat reconciled. John arranged to provide him with rent-free accommodation and to make him a small allowance. In

The Boy Who Became a Legend

1968 Alf, now a fifty-five-year-old widower, married nineteen-year-old Pauline Jones by whom he fathered two sons, half-brothers to John: David in 1969 and Robin in 1973.

The final meeting between Alf and John was on John's 30th birthday in 1970 when he and Pauline, with baby David, called on John at Tittenhurst Park where he was living with his second wife, Yoko Ono. John was verbally abusive to them and promptly withdrew all financial support. Alf died in 1976 aged sixty-three. Had John not achieved such wealth and fame as a very high-profile performer, it seems unlikely his father would ever have sought to be reunited and reconciled with the son he had abandoned so many years before.

John never outgrew his anger and bitterness and he carried it with him into adulthood. He poured his feelings into a song, "Working Class Hero", that he wrote and recorded in 1970, when he was aged thirty. Like the song "Mother", it formed part of his first post-Beatles album, *John Lennon /Plastic Ono Band.* Although he was not by upbringing working class, (nor did he pretend to be any kind of a hero), the lyrics of the song, and in particular the first three verses, are very personal to the life of its composer. They are a plaintive cry from John Lennon's heart: a lament on the traumas of his childhood and teenage years that left him so scarred as an adult.

Chapter 30
Little Richard

Notwithstanding all the musical influences on fifteen-year-old John Lennon through the many record playing and sing-along sessions at my house, reinforced and encouraged by his mother with the aid of her little gramophone, John still had no conception in 1956 that a highly successful musical destiny awaited him. It took the raw power of Little Richard's recording of "Long Tall Sally", and my enthusiasm for it, over a surreptitious meal of fish and chips at my house on my return from Amsterdam, to open his eyes to the attraction of becoming a musician himself and to motivate him to take his first step towards making the dream a reality.

John readily acknowledged the influence of Little Richard on his life when he said: "Little Richard was one of the all-time greats. I still love Little Richard. That's the music that brought me from the provinces of England to the world. That's what made me what I am. I had no idea of doing music as a way of life until rock 'n' roll hit me. That's the music that inspired me to play music."

He could hardly have been any more specific. Most of John Lennon's biographers have failed to identify and write about how John was influenced through me, by Little Richard, to take

The Boy Who Became a Legend

up music as a way of life. We have already heard the graphic descriptions of these triggers by John's best friend, Pete Shotton.

In his book, *The Lives of John Lennon,* Albert Goldman wrote:

"Though the impact of Elvis on John's life was total, he was forced to recognise that there were better rock 'n' roll singers. At the same time that he discovered Elvis, he made an even more momentous discovery: Little Richard. The boy at whose home John first heard Richard was Mike Hill, who had a remarkable collection of American records, including all the great early rhythm and blues singers. Since Hill lived very near school and had a working mother, he was able to entertain John and his friends every day at lunch.

'This boy at school (Mike Hill) had been to Holland,' recalled Lennon. 'He said he'd got this record by someone who was better than Elvis. Elvis was bigger than religion in my life. We used to go to Mike's house and listen to Elvis on 78s. We'd buy five senior Service (cheap cigarettes) loose in the shop (actually they were Players Weights) and some chips and we'd go along. The new record was 'Long Tall Sally' (B-side 'Slippin' and Slidin''). When I heard it, it was so great I couldn't speak. You know how you are torn. I didn't want to leave Elvis. We all looked at each other, but I didn't want to say anything against Elvis, not even in my mind. How could they be happening in my life, both of them? And then someone, (it was Pete Shotton) said, 'It's a Negro singing.' So Elvis was white, and Little Richard was black. 'Thank you God', I said. There was a difference between them. But I thought about it for days at school, and of the labels on the records. One was yellow (Little Richard), and one was blue (Elvis), and I thought of the yellow against the blue.'"

By the time John gave this interview in 1969 to the journalist, Maureen Cleave, writing for the *London Evening Standard*, he had already achieved phenomenal fame with The Beatles and many eventful years had passed since that lunchtime at my house back in 1956. That he had such a clear recall of the life-changing moment when he first heard Little Richard's "Long Tall Sally", even down to the colour of the record label, demonstrates the impact it had on him. He was never the same from that moment on.

The very amateurish skiffle group that John and the others formed at Quarry Bank High School in Liverpool in 1956, and which eventually became the highly professional Beatles, came close to falling apart on more than one occasion. As noted, out of the original six young men in the group, all but John dropped out, one by one, to concentrate on their studies or because they lost interest. None of the five that dropped out had ever contemplated becoming a full-time musician. Only John had that career ambition from the group's early days. He never lost sight of it, and he didn't appear to worry too much about the risky prospects it seemed to offer. The other original members regarded being in the group as simply a fun thing to do, as a pastime in their teens.

Soon after Paul McCartney met John Lennon in July 1957 at the church fete in Woolton where The Quarry Men were performing, he agreed to join John's group. Once he actually did this, in October 1957, the transition from skiffle group to rock 'n' roll group accelerated. By the end of 1959, with the then sixteen-year-old George Harrison in the group, The Quarry Men name and the skiffle had gone. So too had all the original group members, other than John Lennon. The Beatles were on their way but their success was far from assured and it would take another three years before, 'with a little help from their friends', they burst out into the world popular music scene. When they did, they proceeded to rewrite the book.

As fate would have it, the Liverpool College of Art, at which John was enrolled, was located right next-door to the Liverpool Institute, the grammar school where the newly recruited member of John's Quarry Men, Paul McCartney, who was one school year behind John, had just started his fifth and potentially final year. Paul's subsequent decision to stay on at school in the sixth form for two more years after completing his fifth school year, meant that John's almost three years at the art school coincided with Paul's final three years at the next-door grammar school.

John Lennon:

So, for this three-year period, these two budding songwriters and musicians were able to meet frequently and to develop their musical collaboration. They usually did this at the art school during lunch breaks, or when they both skipped a lesson or two.

Paul's younger friend, George Harrison, was also at the Liverpool Institute but was only in his fourth year, one school year below Paul. When he too joined The Quarry Men a year later in 1958, the three young musicians would practise together at the art school or, in fine weather, outdoors in the nearby graveyard alongside the massive Anglican Cathedral. Sometimes they would take the afternoon off and take the corporation bus down to Paul's house at 20, Forthlin Road in Allerton, where they took over the small front room for their practise sessions.

Like all UK teenagers, John had expected to be called up for two years of compulsory military service on reaching the age of eighteen, which in his case was in October 1958. But, fortunately for him, the UK Government had recently abolished the call-up for all those born after 30 September 1939. This meant John and I both missed being drafted by just one year. Had John been called up for national service, most likely into the army, it could well have spelled the end of The Quarry Men/ Beatles and, at the very least, would have curtailed the fruitful Lennon/ McCartney/ Harrison musical co-operation. As it was, the three years these three up-and-coming musicians were able to practise together, while they attended adjacent schools, were critical to the survival and ultimate success of the group.

As The Quarry Men slowly metamorphosed into The Beatles, and as the dynamic and original group, that was destined to achieve unprecedented and long-lasting fame, was forged in the crucible of Hamburg's notorious Reeperbahn nightclubs, it was Little Richard's music that they constantly played rather than anything by Elvis Presley or others. The enormous impact on the group of Little Richard, and in particular of his song "Long Tall Sally" became increasingly apparent.

The man himself, Richard Penniman, better known as Little Richard, had been born in 1932 in Georgia in the Deep South of the segregated United States during the great depression. He was one of twelve children in the poverty-stricken family of a black Seventh Day Adventist preacher, who was also a bar owner and bootlegger, and who was later murdered.

There are some interesting parallels between Little Richard's family and John's family. Little Richard was working as a dishwasher in Los Angeles in 1955 when he recorded his first hit record, "Tutti Frutti", for Specialty Records. This was also the occupation at that time of John Lennon's long lost itinerant father, Alf Lennon. In another parallel, John Lennon's namesake grandfather had been a black and white minstrel. So too had Little Richard. But whereas John at the age of fifteen was just taking the first tentative steps of his musical career, Little

Richard at the same age was already performing regularly with Sugarfoot Sam's Minstrel Show.

It was Little Richard, more than any other performer, who created rock 'n' roll from its gospel music and black rhythm and blues roots. He had been singing gospel music from a very young age, and had developed a manic performing style. His powerful singing voice screamed out the lyrics, and his wild piano playing even included using his feet on the keyboard. His hairstyle was as flamboyant as his mode of dress. All of this made a great impression on generations of fans. This was rock 'n' roll in the raw.

Paul McCartney, being almost two years younger than John, was only thirteen years old when Little Richard's "Long Tall Sally" was released in March 1956, as compared with John's age at the time of fifteen. The record didn't have the instant life-changing impact on him that it had had on John.

Nevertheless, it did impress him when he eventually heard it and he included it as one of the songs he practised playing and singing. Out of all the songs he could have selected from his repertoire to play for John when he auditioned for him in St. Peter's Church Hall in July 1957, he could hardly have chosen one more likely to impress him than "Long Tall Sally". Of course, he had no knowledge then of the special place this held in John's affection given it had triggered his decision less than a year and a half before to become a rock 'n' roll musician.

The Boy Who Became a Legend

Although John had such a strong affection for "Long Tall Sally", the fact was that Paul could sing it, unlike John, who couldn't reach Little Richard's range. Once these two teenagers combined their musical talents, Paul soon absorbed John's enthusiasm for Little Richard with the result that he made "Long Tall Sally" his own special number in the group's live performances and slammed it out in authentic Little Richard style. John was happy enough to let him do this, and he in turn made his version of the Isley Brothers' "Twist and Shout" his own manic specialty.

Both of these songs went right back to the early days of their group experience and both of them were hollering rock 'n' roll numbers. On their concert tours, The Beatles usually performed only a dozen numbers in a very short show. It became the norm for John to get things off to a rocking start with his 'give it all you've got' rendition of "Twist and Shout" and for Paul to close the show by singing his unashamed copy of Little Richard's "Long Tall Sally".

In May 1960, the group, still part-time musicians and calling themselves The Silver Beatles, undertook their first tour engagement, travelling around Scotland as a backing group for the singer Johnny Gentle, performing mostly in ballrooms. They came on stage first as a solo warm-up act and the six numbers they did were mostly hits by Little Richard.

John Lennon:

At this point the group didn't have a regular drummer and was still a raw amateur group. Tommy Moore, a part-time drummer, was hired for this tour. Tommy had a daytime job as a forklift driver at the Garston Bottle Works. After taking time off work to do the tour, he soon refused to play with the group again, and recalled; "Lennon once told me he'd commit suicide rather than get a conventional job. 'Death before work', were his very words." This was while Paul was still in the sixth form at grammar school and John was still attending, when he felt like it, the classes at the art school.

John's employment prospects were no better than they had been when he left grammar school. At the art school he was always close to being expelled on account of missing classes, failing to complete assignments and failing to pass examinations. He finally drifted away from the school before completion of his three-year course, but even had he held on to the end, he would have failed to obtain any qualifications that might have helped him find a position in the art world. Fortunately, thanks to club owner and manager Allan Williams, who got The Beatles to Hamburg, and to the manager the group later appointed, Brian Epstein, John was finally able to achieve his ambition of earning a living as a full-time musician and songwriter.

By January 1962 the group, now full-time professionals, known simply as The Beatles, and with their performance dramatically improved after two arduous and intensive

The Boy Who Became a Legend

performance contracts in Hamburg, had built up a big fan following in Liverpool and the wider area of Merseyside. Thanks to Brian Epstein's efforts, they had started to get higher billing.

In October 1962 the four Beatles, Lennon, McCartney and Harrison on guitars plus Ringo Starr, who had replaced Pete Best on drums, were able not only to meet, but also to perform on the same bill with their inspiration, Little Richard, who had just returned to performing after several years spent pursuing his religious interests. The Beatles first shared the bill with him on 12 October at a concert in the historic New Brighton Tower Ballroom, across the River Mersey from Liverpool, then again on 28 October at the famous Liverpool Empire Theatre. The first meeting the boys had with Little Richard was a real thrill for them, unlike their somewhat disappointing meeting three years later with the inarticulate Elvis Presley at his house in Los Angeles.

Little Richard.

John Lennon:

The author Hunter Davies, in his 1968 authorised biography *The Beatles*, wrote: "John dug out and gave me an old programme for a bill they had been on in 1962 as a supporting group to Little Richard. On the front of the programme John had secured Little Richard's autograph, as any ordinary fan might do, plus his address in USA in case John might visit America one day. At the time it had seemed a remote possibility."

In November 1962, on their fourth and penultimate trip to Hamburg, performing at the big Star-Club, The Beatles, now recording artists were again second billing to Little Richard. John remembered "how thrilled we were, the four of us, even to see any great rock 'n' roller in the flesh and we were almost paralysed with adoration. We used to sit backstage at Hamburg's Star-Club and watch Little Richard play. I still love him. He's one of the greatest." Ringo Starr recalled: "I watched Little Richard at the Star-Club twice a night for six days. It was so great."

Sixteen-year-old Hammond B3 organist Billy Preston was part of Little Richard's road band, the Upsetters, for those Hamburg shows. He had been playing gospel music in the US since the tender age of ten but was new to rock 'n' roll. He remembered the big impact Little Richard had on The Beatles. "Little Richard had been their idol for years. In Hamburg they'd always be with him, asking him questions about America, the cities, the stars, the movies, Elvis and all that." Billy Preston later settled in England and provided keyboard backing on some Beatles' studio recordings. He also played with The Rolling Stones, among others. After The Beatles broke up, he backed John and Yoko Ono in the Plastic Ono Band as well as George Harrison as a solo performer. He died in 2006 aged fifty-nine.

Little Richard himself recalled that during their time performing together in Hamburg, "they'd come to my dressing room and eat there every night. They hadn't any money so I paid for their food. I used to buy steaks for John. Paul would come in, sit down and just look at me. He wouldn't move his eyes. And he'd say 'Oh Richard! You're my idol. Just let me touch you.' He wanted to learn my little holler, so we sat at the piano going ooooh until he got it." The famous oooohs in "She Loves You" and in other Beatles' hits are a direct copy of the ones by Little Richard in "Long Tall Sally".

The enormous significance of "Long Tall Sally" in motivating John Lennon to take up music as a career, and of Little Richard's performances on and off stage as an inspiration to The Beatles, cannot be over-emphasised. Besides usually warming up with Little Richard numbers before a live performance or a recording session, The Beatles featured "Long Tall Sally" in their concerts more prominently than any other number.

In the very first concert of their first US tour on 11 February 1964 at the Coliseum in Washington DC, the history-making show ended with "Long Tall Sally". The last show of their third and final US tour on 29 August 1966 at San Francisco's Candlestick Park also ended with "Long Tall Sally".

It seems entirely fitting that John Lennon's musical journey as the concert-performing founder and leader of The Beatles, that began in the lounge room of my house in Liverpool in 1956 with "Long Tall Sally", should end, a tumultuous decade later in 1966 in San Francisco, with the very same song being performed as the final number in what turned out to be the last ever Beatles concert. The wheel had, indeed, turned full circle.

This last live performance by The Beatles of "Long Tall Sally" was the group's way of acknowledging the singer, and the song, that had inspired John Lennon, Paul McCartney and the other Beatles through their song writing, recording and over 1,400 live performances, and taken them into the hearts of millions of people all around the world.

Even after The Beatles finally disbanded, and while John was still living in England, it was the inclusion of Little Richard in the line-up for the Toronto Rock 'n' Roll Revival Show in September 1969 that influenced John Lennon to decide, at the last moment, to fly over to Canada to take part in the show, and to break his self-imposed embargo on live performances.

Paul McCartney too didn't forget his Little Richard roots in his post-Beatles musical career. In 1973, his new group Wings

The Boy Who Became a Legend

brought the shows in their first UK tour to a rocking finale with a medley of raw rock 'n' roll hits of Little Richard.

The very last live stage performance by John Lennon was at New York's Hilton Hotel on 18 April 1975 when he recorded, for television, an ATV special. He performed only three numbers. The final one of these was once again a Little Richard number, and a very significant one too. He performed "Slippin' and Slidin'", the B-side of the record "Long Tall Sally" that was burned into his psyche when he first heard both sides of it at my house in Liverpool in 1956.

John knew exactly what he was doing when he selected this as the last song for his final live performance, out of the many thousands that were available to him. He was bringing his performing career to a close by acknowledging the same Little Richard record that had triggered it off nineteen years before.

John never thanked me personally for helping to get his musical career started although, to be fair, I hadn't made it any the easier for him to do so by leaving England in 1963 to work and live in Central Asia, and then emigrating to Australia in 1970. However, once he scaled the dizzying heights up to the predicted 'toppermost of the poppermost', he did give me the credit in media interviews for having triggered the start of his musical career. I like to think that the number he selected to close his short final performance before a small live audience in

New York in 1975 was his way, perhaps subconsciously, of closing the circle.

Lonnie Donegan, Elvis Presley, Hank Williams, Chuck Berry and Buddy Holly, among others, all had an influence on John Lennon and The Beatles. But the most significant influence of all was, without a doubt, Little Richard. As I write this book in 2012, Little Richard is aged eighty, still performs occasionally, and lives in Nashville, Tennessee. His pivotal role in the history of John Lennon and The Beatles deserves to be much more widely understood and acknowledged.

Chapter 31

Divergence

Our lives, John Lennon's and mine, had run on close parallel tracks for twelve formative years, from the age of five to almost seventeen. But once we both left Quarry Bank High School in July 1957, the paths of our lives rapidly diverged as we moved towards the fulfilment of our distinctly different destinies.

While John was being himself, fooling around at the art school, as he had fooled around at the grammar school, and wondering what he was doing stuck in the lettering class, that held no interest for him, I was working not very far away in the city centre of Liverpool in the office of Bent's Brewery, and learning the principles of double entry accounting in a bookkeeping course at night school. Armed with my six GCE passes, I was on the lookout for a job with better prospects and wider horizons than of becoming an area manager of public houses for a local brewery.

By good fortune, through a friend of my mother, I found my job and my future career in a company called Reliance Marine Insurance Company Limited, where I started in November 1957 as a junior in the Overseas Department in the company's Water Street office. This was opposite India Buildings, a block down from the Liverpool Town Hall and only a short walk to The Cavern in Mathew Street off North John Street, which, although he didn't know it at the time, John Lennon (and The Beatles) would later make world-famous.

Pete Shotton was also at something of a loss as to what to do with himself after leaving school. He surprised us all, and especially his best friend John, by enrolling as a police cadet–hardly a career any of us would have expected him to choose or to be accepted for, given his general anti-authority attitude to life. He did eventually qualify as a policeman, but quit soon afterwards as he found the work didn't suit him. He then went on to manage a late night coffee bar called the Old Dutch Café on Smithdown Road. In my early twenties I met Pete there on several occasion in the early hours of the morning, after a night on the town. In those days it was one of the very few places open in Liverpool at that time of night, and was a meeting place for all sorts of characters, some of them on the wrong side of the law.

Within six years of leaving grammar school, John, Pete and I had all become part of the Liverpool Diaspora and would never live in the city again. In fact we would all end up living overseas; John in New York, Pete in Dublin and me in Melbourne, Australia. But, as expatriates, we each remained proud of our Liverpool origins.

The Boy Who Became a Legend

As the skiffle craze rapidly faded away in the late 1950s, and as rock 'n' roll continued its inexorable climb, The Quarry Men, with John Lennon still as leader, slowly metamorphosed into The Beatles, with John and Paul McCartney as the songwriters and guitar-playing lead singers, George Harrison also on guitar, John's art school friend, Stuart Sutcliffe, on bass guitar, with Pete Best on drums. These were the members of The Beatles when they had what proved to be their professional breakthrough in August 1960 as, thanks to the owner of the Jacaranda Coffee Bar, Allan Williams, they went overseas for the first time to play for several months at a club in the notorious red-light district of the North German city of Hamburg. They became very popular in the Hamburg clubs and returned there to play on four more occasions.

Had they been looking for a foreign city with many of the same characteristics as the tough port city of Liverpool, they couldn't have done better than to choose Hamburg. They enjoyed living there, despite their poor living conditions and low pay. Looking back on those days, they acknowledged that they grew up in Hamburg, in a personal as well as in a musical and professional sense. Sadly, Stuart Sutcliffe, after falling in love with a local girl, Astrid Kirchherr, dropping out of the group and settling in Hamburg, died there not long afterwards. Of the remaining four, Pete Best was precipitately dismissed and replaced by Ringo Starr, just at the very moment in August 1962 when the group started to record and began their meteoric

John Lennon:

climb to unimagined fame and unprecedented commercial success.

During this time, and until I left England in August 1963 to work and live overseas, I used to see ex-Quarry Bank friends, particularly Don Beattie, Roy Bradley and John Turner. We met, at least every Friday, for an evening of beer drinking and camaraderie and congregated in a small pub opposite St John's Market in town. After a few pints of brown mixed (half a pint of mild beer plus a bottle of brown ale), we liked to sing the mostly dirty rugby club type songs that one or other of us would introduce, or to which we could contribute new verses. Between us, we developed an extensive repertoire. Unlike John's singing, ours was purely for fun and never taken seriously.

Several times in the year after we left Quarry Bank High School in July 1957, Don and I went to Paul McCartney's house to catch up with our friend John Lennon, and to watch and listen to The Quarry Men rehearsing in the small front living room. People came and went and, with the musicians and hangers-on, there was hardly room to swing the proverbial cat. None of us had the slightest prescience of the amazing future that awaited the budding musical partnership of Lennon and McCartney.

We gradually saw less and less of John and Pete Shotton after that, as we were increasingly moving in different circles, but we used to see them now and again. They both came to several of the parties I had at my house, and my attractive next-door neighbour, Denise Wickens, as she was then, clearly recalls meeting John at one of those parties. "He wasn't at all sociable and used to sit in the corner of the room not joining in: an angry young man. Pete was a lot more outgoing than John. My friend Doreen Warren dated John and found him very sullen." That would have been soon after his mother was so tragically killed in July 1958 and John was embittered by her death.

Quite some time later, with John Turner, who also worked in a city office, I went to The Cavern during lunchtime to listen to the group, and to catch up with John. This was early in 1961, following their return from Hamburg, energised and hardened by their experience. It was from then, and through 1961 and 1962, that The Beatles built their reputation around Merseyside as the top local rock 'n' roll group. During this two-year period, they played four more times in Hamburg, and appointed Brian Epstein as their manager in December 1961.

Not having been to The Cavern since it had changed from a jazz club to a rock 'n' roll club, we were shocked to discover that the average age of the girls in the lunchtime audience was around fifteen. We felt quite ancient, even though we were only twenty at the time. I guess I had forgotten that I was only sixteen when I went to The Cavern for the first time.

We really enjoyed the music, and the black leather-clad group put on a captivating show. It was easy to sense the sexual

John Lennon:

excitement generated in the largely young female audience. We felt a bit out of place in our business suits as we chatted to John in his black leather outfit, but being lunchtime in a busy commercial city, there were plenty of other young men similarly dressed.

Chapter 32

Taking Off

After their coming of age in Hamburg, both musically and psychologically, and now 'battle-hardened' professionals after the relentless pressure to perform long hours for tough club audiences, The Beatles, when Brian Epstein first met them in a sweaty cellar in Liverpool, were already a top Merseyside group with a growing and loyal fan base.

It is debatable what attracted Brian to propose becoming their manager. It certainly wasn't their music–Brian preferred classical music. It might have been the commercial opportunity that he thought he could see but more likely it was the sexual aura of the four rough-looking black leather clad young men that excited and attracted him as a homosexual with a liking for the rough trade. Be that as it may, they needed a manager and were glad to accept Brian, even though he had no qualifications for the job.

In 1962, thanks largely to Brian Epstein's efforts, The Beatles really started to climb the ladder of success. He was about to launch the four Liverpool lads on an unsuspecting public, in the UK initially, and then in Europe, the US and the rest of the world. He had met a lot of resistance in trying to interest record companies in this unknown Merseyside group. But his persistence paid off and in June of 1962 The Beatles signed their longed-for recording contract with EMI's Parlophone label, and in September in London, under the sure guidance of producer George Martin, they recorded their first record, "Love Me Do" backed by "P.S. I Love You". This was released on 5 October 1962 and it got the group into the UK Top Twenty for the first time. In November 1962, they travelled to Hamburg to perform there for the fifth time.

1963 started with a bang for The Beatles and, from that point, the momentum just accelerated. On 11 January their second single, "Please Please Me" backed by "Ask Me Why", was released, and by 22 February it had reached the number one position in the UK Top Twenty. Their highly acclaimed first long play album, also titled *Please Please Me,* was released on 22 March, having been recorded in a single 11-hour marathon session.

With supporting TV appearances and one live show after another in the UK, their feet hardly touched the ground. The Beatles were up, up and away. The press latched on to this new phenomenon in a big way and, after their show at the London Palladium on 13 October 1963, came up with the word 'Beatlemania' to describe the frenzied reception from the largely young female audiences that greeted their every appearance, and largely drowned out their music at live shows.

The Boy Who Became a Legend

It was not only the four Beatles and their manager who were amazed at this meteoric rise to unimagined success. So too were their families and their childhood friends, myself included. I was thrilled by what was happening and we all wished them well.

Just as the careers of John Lennon and the other members of The Beatles took off, so did mine, albeit in a less spectacular way. Unfortunately, it took me a long way away from them; just at the point where their rate of climb to success became stratospheric.

By mid-1963, with five years of marine insurance experience at Reliance Marine Insurance Company in Liverpool and with all my insurance exams completed, I was keen to travel. Having applied to work overseas to gain wider experience, I was assigned, at the age of twenty-two, to the Arabian Gulf to work for five months as the acting manager of the insurance department of a major Kuwaiti trading firm that acted as agent for my British insurance company.

On 2 August 1963, prior to flying off to Cairo and on to Kuwait, I went with several friends who knew John Lennon from our schooldays, to see and hear him performing with The Beatles at the Grafton Rooms in Liverpool. It was a terrific show and the group received a great reception. During intermission, we spoke to John and wished him well. He had just come off stage after singing an all-out rendition of "Twist and Shout". He was smoking heavily and it wasn't surprising that his voice was so hoarse that he could hardly speak. Sadly, this turned out to be the last time we met each other, although I continued to follow his career with the keenest interest.

In January 1964, with my job in Kuwait coming to an end, I accepted, at the age of twenty-three, what promised to be an interesting and challenging career assignment to join two older English colleagues in forming and managing the very first insurance company in Kabul, Afghanistan, to be simply called Afghan Insurance Company. This was to be a joint venture between Guardian Assurance and Afghan investors and would be the first British investment in remote Afghanistan. The company turned out to be highly successful, which, sadly, is more than can be said for the country.

So, after two weeks holiday en route from Kuwait to Liverpool, which took me to Egypt, Jordan, Lebanon, Cyprus and Turkey, and a further fortnight in England, I found myself early in February 1964 in Kabul, amid the deep snows of the Hindu Kush mountains in Central Asia at 6,000 feet above sea level–a big contrast to the heat of the Arabian desert only months before. Just as I took off from London in my Pan American jet to Tehran en route to Kabul, The Beatles, with my old friend John Lennon, took off from London too, in their case bound for the first of their appearances in the USA, to be followed by three tumultuous tours, playing to rapturous receptions from huge audiences.

The Boy Who Became a Legend

John and I were both on the move, physically and career-wise, but unfortunately we were on dramatically diverging paths. Soon we might just as well have been on different planets. Remote Afghanistan was about as far away as you could possibly get from Beatlemania although, while I lived there, I bought all The Beatles' albums by mail order. My mother in Liverpool regularly mailed me cuttings from the *Liverpool Echo* that kept me abreast of the group's activities. They hardly ever seemed to be out of the headlines.

Afghanistan, when I lived there from 1964 to 1969, was progressing from medieval backwardness to the beginnings of a modern state, and from an absolute monarchy to a parliamentary democracy with a king as head of state. The mood was one of optimism while the country received aid and development assistance from many developed countries and from many of the agencies of the United Nations. There was no intimation whatsoever of the violence and horrors that lay ahead for this unlucky country, and which would wreck every aspect of Afghan society, kill and maim many of its citizens, and scatter millions of others around the world as refugees.

By the time I returned to Liverpool two and a half years later, in August 1966, on my first home leave from Afghanistan, The Beatles had already performed the last concert of their third and final tour of the USA. This turned out to be their last concert performance altogether: their touring days were over. From this point, until they disbanded, they were a group only for the purposes of recording.

Having been six years in the making, from the first fumbling notes of The Quarry Men in 1956 to the first record release of The Beatles in 1962, their time 'at the toppermost of the poppermost', to use John's famous phrase, was quite short but intense, creative and spectacular. In his wildest dreams, John could never have imagined 'the top' being, metaphorically speaking, off the planet. The pace of public performances was altogether too hot and too strong to be maintained. But the four Liverpool lads who became, and remain, mega-famous, would continue as a group for a few more years and produce some outstanding recordings, including the classic and groundbreaking *Sergeant Pepper* album.

On my way from Kabul to Liverpool on home leave in 1966, I had collected a new Volkswagen Beetle car from the factory at Wolfsburg, near Hannover in Germany, and after spending two months in UK, I drove the car all the way from there back to my home in Kabul, through fifteen countries in thirty days, taking the route through Istanbul, Beirut, Damascus, Baghdad and Tehran.

While I was living once again in Kabul, I read in the papers that The Beatles were to travel to India for an extended period of meditation. This motivated me to write to John, to let him know I was living in Afghanistan and to invite him to come and stay with me after leaving India, seeing that Kabul was on the route back to England. I never received a reply to my letter and most likely it was lost amid piles of fan mail and never read by John or brought to his attention. This was a pity, as I felt sure he would have loved Kabul and its hippie culture and ready availability of marijuana–it was the perfect place in those peaceful days for a Beatle to chill out!

After finally leaving Afghanistan in May 1969, and travelling for two months as far as Japan, then across the USSR on the Trans-Siberian Railway, and through still-communist Eastern Europe, I had a few months in London where I got married, and accepted, with the same UK based employer, an attractive job in Melbourne, Australia, and emigrated there in January 1970.

So, once again, John and I were headed off in very different directions; he the following year to the USA with Yoko Ono to live in New York, until his murder in 1980, and me to Australia for a rewarding career in marine insurance, and to start a family.

I never forgot my close friendship with John throughout our school years and wondered if one day we would meet again: but it never happened. Like millions around the world, I was shocked and greatly saddened by the news of his murder in December 1980.

As the years went by, John continued to live on for me, and for so many other people. The appreciation of his life and his music has grown, rather than diminished, since his death, and has attracted legions of new fans who were too young, or not even born, during the Beatle years, and during John's years of post-Beatles work. His music is still heard regularly on the radio and even in supermarkets. Hardly a month goes by without news or media coverage of one or other of The Beatles, or without hearing their music.

If "Imagine" were the only song that John Lennon ever wrote, he would be assured of eternal fame, just as Paul McCartney would be for his song "Yesterday". As it is, many of the songs these two composers wrote, in collaboration and alone, have already become standards. The music they made with George Harrison and Ringo Starr as The Beatles still sounds good today, after fifty years.

I had put right at the back of my mind my memories of growing up with John, and of my key role in his decision to take up music as a career. But in the year 2000, quite unexpectedly, all this history sprang back to life again in an extraordinary way that was to bring happy consequences for me. Not the least of these has been to reconnect me with the spirit of John Lennon. I have felt his presence particularly strongly during the course of writing this book. It has been so good to feel close to John again after all these years.

Chapter 33

A Fascinating Photo

How I came to reconnect with John Lennon in the year 2000, and the impact this had on my life, is a story in itself. My elderly widowed mother in Liverpool, Beryl Hill, was an avid reader of the regional Merseyside newspaper, the *Liverpool Echo*. She used to cut out any item she saw that she thought might interest me and enclose it with one of her regular letters to me in Australia. When carefully reading through the paper one day in late 1989, her eyes lit upon an article about Dovedale Road County Primary School which she remembered I had attended between 1945 and 1952, so she cut it out and sent it on to me. The article was about a retired teacher, and included a photo of one of his old classes.

When I looked at the newspaper article, I saw the photo wasn't of my class. However, the teacher, Fred Bolt, who taught in the junior section of the school from 1947 to 1973, was the only teacher of whom I had a clear recollection and who I still remembered with affection after all the years since I had left the school. In the article, he appealed to his old pupils to write to him about their lives as adults. I resolved to do just that. So, one evening in February 1990, I sat down at my study bench in my home in Melbourne and prepared to write a letter to my old schoolteacher, who I had last seen when I left his school at the age of eleven, and with whom I'd had no contact in over forty years.

As I prepared to put pen to paper, I found myself faced with a strange dilemma. How should I begin the letter? Should I start with Dear Sir, as I used to address him when I was an eleven-year-old, or Dear Mr. Bolt? Deciding both of these were too formal, I settled on the more relaxed Australian style of Dear Fred, and wrote him a summary of my life since the age of eleven and of my present circumstances.

I received an appreciative reply from Fred Bolt, with which he enclosed brief details of what those members of my 1952 leaving class who had been in contact with him, had made of their lives. This I found very interesting. It included the information that a good friend of mine from Dovedale Road School days, Tim Holmes, with whom I'd totally lost touch, was living in Chester, not far from Liverpool, and working as a piano tuner.

Having re-established contact with each other, Fred and I exchanged news and greetings at Christmas each year, then in 1995, as I had to go to London on business, I wrote to Fred and arranged to meet him. I stayed a few days with my mother in Liverpool; then we drove to Nottingham to spend the night with a cousin of mine. On our way there, we visited Fred, who was living in Walsall near Birmingham, and took him out to lunch. It was very strange to meet him again after such a long time. I immediately recognised him, but I don't think there was any way he could see, in the fifty-four-year-old man who greeted him, the eleven-year-old boy he had taught a lifetime ago. Anyway, we got along well, and after our reunion we continued to exchange the occasional letter and greetings at Christmas.

A few months after our meeting in 1995, Fred, who had been widowed for several years, moved to live with his sister in Weston-super-Mare in Somerset. In the last letter I received from him, just prior to Christmas in 1999, he wrote about how he had recently been to the theatre in Weston-super-Mare and had enjoyed a variety show starring the famous–at least in the UK–comedian, Jimmy Tarbuck, who was one of his old pupils at Dovedale Road School.

Before the show, Fred's sister, unbeknown to him, had contacted the theatre to advise that Jimmy's old primary school teacher would be attending that evening's performance. The management must have passed this information on to Jimmy, as, during the show, Fred was surprised, but delighted, when Jimmy acknowledged his presence in the audience. Considering this was the same teacher who's discipline of Jimmy had caused him, as an eleven-year-old in 1951 to run away from the school camp in the Isle of Man, it was just as well Jimmy wasn't still harbouring a grudge.

John Lennon:

After the performance, Fred and his sister were invited backstage to meet Jimmy Tarbuck. When they were introduced to Jimmy, Fred's sister presented him with an enlargement print she had had made, without Fred's knowledge, of a tiny black and white photo that Fred had taken almost fifty years before on his simple Kodak Brownie 127 Bakelite box camera.

The photo showed the two most famous old boys of Dovedale Road School, ten-year-old John Lennon and eleven-year-old Jimmy Tarbuck, standing next to each other at the front of a group of schoolboys in their bathing costumes at the same school camp in the Isle of Man back in 1951 that Jimmy Tarbuck later ran away from. This photo was one of a series taken by Fred on that holiday.

In January 2000, a month after Fred wrote to me about his reunion with Jimmy Tarbuck, I had to attend a meeting at the office of Lloyd's in London, of the Executive Committee of the International Union of Marine Insurance (the global trade association for marine insurance), of which I was at the time a member and a vice-chairman. I had arranged, during my journey back to Australia from England, to make short business calls on clients of my company in the Maldives, Papua New Guinea and Solomon Islands.

One night during this journey, while I was flying high above the Indian Ocean, heading from the Maldives to Singapore in transit to Papua New Guinea, my wife June, back in Melbourne, received an unusual phone call from England very late at night from a young lady journalist from the newspaper, the *Daily Mail*, wanting to speak to Michael Hill about a photograph of him with John Lennon and Jimmy Tarbuck. My wife explained my absence, and then did her best to answer the journalist's questions. When I phoned her the next day from Port Moresby in Papua New Guinea, she told me about this strange phone call. I was quite mystified, particularly as the journalist hadn't explained where and when the photo was taken. I said I wasn't aware of the existence of any such photo. We went on to talk about other matters, and I put the story about the mysterious phone call from the UK out of my mind.

However, a few days later, on the first morning back at my office after returning to Australia, several phone calls from the media alerted me to the publication in the UK of an old photo, in which I apparently appeared standing behind John Lennon and Jimmy Tarbuck in a group of ten and eleven-year-old boys on a beach. I realised this must be the same photo that the UK journalist had wanted to discuss with me a few days earlier when I was travelling, and I learned it had been taken forty-nine years before, in 1951, during the Dovedale Road School holiday in the Isle of Man.

During the course of the day, I was interviewed in my office by a journalist from the *Melbourne Herald Sun* newspaper and was the subject of a feature article explaining my pivotal role in turning John Lennon onto rock 'n' roll. Within the next few days, I appeared in the leading UK shipping and marine insurance paper, *Lloyd's List*, and in the popular magazine, *That's Life*. I also gave a half hour radio interview on a local radio station answering questions from a panel of four excited adult male Beatle fans about my role in John Lennon's life.

All of this was so totally unexpected. There are very few photos of John Lennon as a child, and there had never been one linking John Lennon with Jimmy Tarbuck, and linking me with the two friends of my schooldays who had each grown-up to become famous entertainers. The news value of such a previously unknown photo hadn't been recognised by Fred Bolt but it quickly was by others, once its existence became known.

Over the next few days it gradually became apparent to me what had happened. I learned that, sadly, Fred Bolt had just died at the age of 86, and it transpired that a retired teacher colleague of his, who was aware that Fred's sister had an old and hitherto unknown photo of the two famous old boys of Dovedale Road School, tipped off the *Liverpool Daily Post*. The people there immediately recognised its national news value and handed it on to their senior sister publication, the *Daily Mirror*. One of their people obtained a copy of the photo from Fred's sister and it was published in the paper on 27 January 2000.

The Boy Who Became a Legend

Dovedale Junior School boys in the Isle of Man 1951, taken by Fred Bolt. John Lennon is centre left with arms outstretched. Jimmy Tarbuck is at John's left in a boxing stance. Ivan Vaughan is at Jimmy's left. The author is standing directly behind Jimmy and Ivan–the tall boy with the big grin.

In its full-page article, the *Daily Mirror* wrote only about the two celebrities, Lennon and Tarbuck, standing side by side at the front of the group of boys. The body language of these two destined to be famous boys shown in the photo is very revealing of their characters. Jimmy Tarbuck is captured by the camera in a typical cheeky pose in a fighting stance, with a big grin and with his fists raised at his teacher, Fred Bolt, who was taking the photo. John Lennon, having deliberately positioned himself right at the front centre of the group of boys, has both of his arms outstretched as if to say; 'Keep back. I am the leader.' He is specifically holding back his rival, Jimmy Tarbuck.

When they decided to publish the just discovered photo, the *Daily Mirror* people had only been able to identify Lennon and Tarbuck, both so well known to readers in the UK, among the group of six young boys whose faces were visible. So, in the accompanying article, they posed the question 'Are you one of the unidentified boys in this photo, or do you know who they are?' Another leading popular UK tabloid newspaper, the *Daily Mail*, immediately took up the challenge of identifying the other boys.

Within 24 hours, the people at the *Daily Mail*, in a smart bit of journalism, managed not only to identify each of the four unidentified boys in the old photograph, but also to obtain a photo of each of them as an adult, and biographical details of their adult lives. On 28 January 2000, only a day after the *Daily Mirror* article, the *Daily Mail*, in a double-page spread, published an enlarged version of the nearly fifty-year-old school holiday photograph, with an individual photo of each of the boys as an adult, and a write-up on each of them.

It was revealed that the boy in the photo standing at the other side of Jimmy Tarbuck was John Lennon's friend and mine, Ivan Vaughan. Remember, it was Ivan who, six years after this group photo was taken, introduced Paul McCartney to John Lennon at the Woolton church fete where The Quarry Men were playing, without which the group, had it survived at all, would have been very different from The Beatles and would almost certainly never have become so successful. This is even more the case when it is recalled that it was Paul McCartney in turn who later brought his younger school friend, George Harrison, who John would otherwise never have met, into John's group, then still called The Quarry Men.

The photo also revealed a young me, standing directly behind John Lennon, Jimmy Tarbuck and Ivan Vaughan–the tall boy with the big happy grin on his face. There was no need for me to have been concerned about being in the second row of the group of boys, given my height.

Tim Holmes, my good friend from Dovedale Road School, learned of Fred's death and saw the double-page spread in the *Daily Mail*. He thoughtfully decided to send me a copy of the newspaper. Having, like me, been in contact with Fred, and having met him and his sister, he was able to get my address from her. When I received the newspaper from Tim, I was fascinated to see this historic photo of me with John Lennon and Jimmy Tarbuck, the existence of which had been unknown for almost fifty years, except to the retired schoolmaster who had taken it, and his family and close friends.

Initially, I was puzzled as to how the people at the *Daily Mail* had been able to identify me, trace my phone number in Australia, and get hold of a photo of me as an adult. I discovered later that Tim Holmes had provided them with my contact details. These included my Melbourne address and phone number, and details of the company of which I was at the

John Lennon: time the managing director, Associated Marine Insurers. They then downloaded my photo from the company's website.

Chapter 34

Reconnecting

A number of happy consequences for me were to ensue after the appearance, completely out of the blue, of this historic photo, and its publication in the UK newspapers. The first of these was to reunite me with Tim Holmes, of whom I retained fond memories of childhood friendship. Six months later, he and his lovely wife, Margaret, who as it happened had already arranged to visit Australia, came to stay at my house in Melbourne, for what proved, for both Tim and I, to be a very happy reunion. We resumed our friendship as if there had been no break of fifty years, and we have maintained it ever since, staying several times as guests in each other's houses, in Chester and Melbourne respectively.

On a visit to Chester in September 2001, I stayed with Tim and Margaret. Another house guest was former Quarry Men banjo player Rod Davis who, at Tim's invitation, had come up from his home near London to meet me for the first time since I left Quarry Bank in 1957.

In 1997, on the fortieth anniversary of the since famous performance of the group at the St Peter's Church fete in Woolton in 1957, 'when Lennon met McCartney', it was Rod who located and brought together all of the original members of the group, including Pete Shotton, so that they could re-form The Quarry Men, and stage a replica performance. Sadly, they were of course without the group's most famous member and founder, John Lennon.

The author (left), with Janet and Rod Davis at their London home.

An unexpected consequence came out of my reunion with Rod Davis in England. Some time after I had returned to Melbourne, I received an email from Rod in which he sought my agreement for him to release my contact details to an acquaintance of his in Dallas, Texas, Mark Naboshek, who was, and remains, a serious collector of Beatles memorabilia, and who wished to contact me. Somewhat mystified, I gave my OK.

I soon received an email from Mark who, after introducing himself, explained that he had travelled to the UK in March

The Boy Who Became a Legend

2001 with Gary Lance, a friend and fellow collector of Beatles memorabilia, on a Beatles nostalgia and collecting tour. From a dealer in Chorley, in the North of England, Mark had bought an original whole-school photo of Quarry Bank High School students and teachers, including John Lennon and friends, taken in 1957, when John was sixteen and was approaching the end of his schooldays.

The photo he bought was one of two whole-school photos that I had sold several months before, through a Sotheby's auction. The other photo was similar to the 1957 one, but was taken in 1955 when John and I were both aged fourteen. The Chorley-based dealer had bought both of them at the auction. The 1957 photo that Mark bought from the dealer was signed 'Michael Hill' on the back.

Mark had contacted Rod, knowing him to be an ex-Quarry Bank boy, to seek his help in identifying some of the 'famous' faces in the photo. Rod did this and then amazed Mark by telling him that one of the boys standing near to John in the photo was Michael Hill and went on to tell him about the record playing sessions in my house and the often overlooked significance of these in the John Lennon story.

It was at that point that Mark told Rod that the photo he had bought was originally the property of Michael Hill. Rod in reply told Mark he was in touch with me. He then contacted me to tell me who had ended up as the owner of one of my two old school photos. When Mark emailed me, he said how excited he was to be able to make contact with the original owner of the Quarry Bank photo that he'd recently bought.

Mark also informed me that another friend of his, Paul Goresh, a keen amateur photographer and a collector of vintage Beatles photographs, had bought my 1955 school photo at the New Jersey *Fest for Beatles Fans*, from the same dealer, shortly after Mark and Gary had returned to the States, and Mark had tipped off Paul as to the availability of this photo. I also learned from Mark that Paul Goresh had gained unsought notoriety by having taken the last photograph ever made of John Lennon. This was on the evening of the day in 1980 when John was murdered. That evening, Paul was waiting outside The Dakota in Manhattan and took a photo of John, who was on his way out with Yoko, in the act of signing an album cover for the deranged man who later that same evening shot him dead when he and Yoko returned home and were just about to walk through The Dakota gates. The murderer remains in jail for his mindless crime.

If Fred Bolt's old photo hadn't led to my reunion with Tim Holmes, and through him with Rod Davis, I would never in turn have made contact with Mark. I thought how strange this all was, as if it was meant to be. My old school photos could have ended up in the hands of anyone in the world and I wouldn't have known. When I offered them for sale through Sotheby's, I could never have envisaged that their sale would lead to me travelling to Texas, at the invitation of the new owner of one of the photos, which I did in September 2002, after attending an international marine insurance conference in New York.

Mark Naboshek with the author in Dallas, 2002.

Mark Naboshek, his family and friends gave me a warm welcome in Dallas. This included a memorable evening spent with Mark and Gary Lance at a traditional Texan rodeo as well as the following day with Mark and his friend, Steve McNutt, touring the sites of Dallas and Fort Worth. That evening, Mark and several of his friends dined with me at a Dallas steakhouse: the friends all shared his passion for The Beatles. They were eager to meet me and were fascinated by the first-hand account I was able to give them of growing up with John Lennon in Liverpool in the 1940s and 1950s.

John Lennon:

Mark proudly showed me his comprehensive, and very professionally presented, collection of Beatles memorabilia, including, as a highlight, the original handwritten set list from the group's first-ever American concert which took place in Washington D.C. on 11 February 1964. This was written out that afternoon by John Lennon on a sheet of Shoreham Hotel notepaper, but taken to the concert by Paul McCartney to remind the group which numbers to play. Mark had bought this historic piece of paper in 1994 from a lady who had been at the concert. A policeman had found it left on top of a speaker after The Beatles had left the stage and he handed it to the lady, who was thirteen at the time. She held on to it for the next thirty years before selling it to Mark for $5,000.

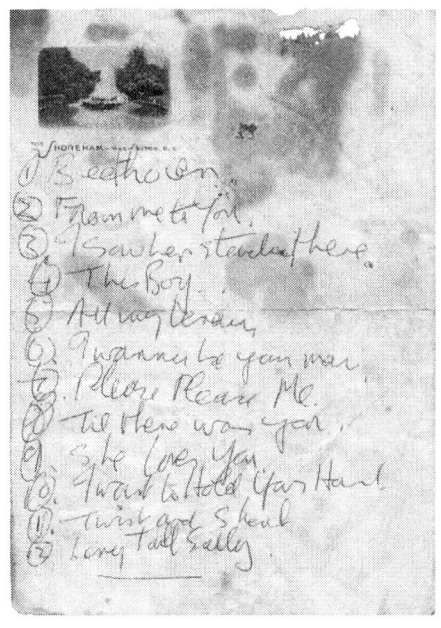

Mark's Beatles Washington D.C. set list

It was Rod Davis who helped me to sell the original Ronnex label Little Richard 78 rpm record of "Long Tall Sally" that played such an important part in the life of John Lennon and in the history of The Beatles and of rock 'n' roll music. On Rod's recommendation, this was sold through a Fleetwood-Owen auction in 2001, with appropriate documents to support its provenance. I never knew who bought this historic item and I would love to know who owns it now, also whether it is on public display. Wherever it is and whoever owns it, I guess its value is likely to be greatly increased by the publication of this book and the resulting wider awareness of its key role in the history of John Lennon and The Beatles.

Most of the other 78rpm records that John Lennon used to listen to in my house between 1954 and 1957, and which did so much to shape his musical development, are now in Mark Naboshek's collection, together with other Quarry Bank High School memorabilia. I felt it was important for all these items to be in the hands of serious collectors, so as to ensure their preservation.

Thanks to Tim Holmes and Rod Davis, I was also able to reconnect with another long lost friend of my youth, Pete Shotton, John's closest friend, and partner in mischief and mayhem, throughout his school years. After his short and aborted career in the police force, Pete had no clear sense of direction in his life. Given the people he was exposed to while working the late shift at Liverpool's Old Dutch Café, he was at a crossroads where, by his own admission, he could have been tempted to follow a criminal path.

John became concerned that, as his fortunes at last were improving, Pete was still drifting. As Pete explained to me when we met, as John finally started to earn serious money, he at one point gave Pete two thousand pounds to help him to start his own business. When they met some time later and John asked him whether he had put the money to good use, Pete replied, "John, I'm sorry but I pissed it all away." At this point many people would have given up on their erstwhile friend, but John, proving what a loyal and true friend he was to Pete, had his accountants look out for a suitable business for his old mate. It was later settled that a supermarket business on Hayling Island, in Hampshire, off the south coast of England, would be bought for Pete by way of an interest-free loan of thirty thousand pounds.

This generous action by John really changed Pete's life, and for the better. It gave him the focus he needed and he proceeded to run the business successfully. Later, when The Beatles founded Apple Corps and decided to open a modern clothing store in London's Baker Street, Pete was engaged to set up and manage it. That it was a financial disaster, like other non-musical ventures of The Beatles, was hardly Pete's fault, with too many impractical and conflicting directions coming from too many people, including individual members of the 'Fab Four'.

Pete had visited the States several times, both during The Beatles' concert tours and later. Through contacts he made there, he obtained, with a business partner, the UK rights for a US steak and foil-wrapped baked potato chain, Fatty Arbuckle's American Diners, and they went on to open, run and franchise a chain of such restaurants. He later bought out his partner, and eventually sold his interest in what he had built up into a successful business. Facing a huge tax bill on the enormous profit from the sale if he remained resident in the UK, he took his tax accountant's advice and became a tax exile in Eire, living in Dublin.

It was in the Hilton Hotel in Dublin, in September 2003, that I finally caught up with Pete, who I had last met at the late night café that he was managing in Liverpool, more than forty years before. Pete seemed as genuinely pleased to meet me again as I was to meet him. We had a few drinks together in my hotel room; then I bought him dinner downstairs in the hotel. He had no money on him–just like the Pete I remembered from our teenage years together! Like many wealthy people, he said he didn't usually carry money on his person. Perhaps that's one of the ways rich people stay rich.

The author (left) with John Lennon's closest friend, Pete Shotton, in Dublin September 2003.

I surprised Pete by giving him a copy of a photo of the two of us, and others, on our memorable school exchange holiday in Amsterdam in 1956. It was so good to reminisce with Pete. Of course we talked mostly about John, and as we did so we both felt his presence very strongly. It was obvious Pete was still grieving for John, the best friend of his youth, and indeed of his life.

When talking about how John had helped him in his life, Pete made a point of telling me how he had repaid to John's widow, Yoko Ono, the whole of the thirty thousand pounds that John had lent him all those years ago as capital for his first business. This was a way for him to honour the memory of John, whose friendship he had held so dear.

Pete and John didn't see much of each other after John left England with Yoko in September 1971, to live in New York. The last time they met was in 1976 in John's apartment at The Dakota. But Pete remained emotionally and spiritually connected to John and was devastated by his murder in 1980. The wound this caused has never really healed and probably never will.

My travelling from Australia to a marine insurance conference in Amsterdam in September 2005, and Tim Holmes' sixty-fifth birthday the same month in England, led to what was for me a memorable meeting with a person who turned out to be someone very special–Julia Baird, half-sister of John Lennon and the oldest daughter of his mother, Julia Lennon, and Bobby Dykins. Julia and I were among the guests who accepted an invitation to attend the birthday party hosted by Tim and Margaret Holmes in their home near Chester.

On meeting Julia, I was immediately struck by her resemblance to her famous half-brother in terms of physical features, hair and glasses. There was no mistaking that this was John's sister. Their common inheritance from their mother was readily apparent.

As John was six and a half years older than Julia, and as she was only ten years old when John left Quarry Bank High

School in 1957 and only eleven when their mother was killed a year later, Julia was keenly interested when we shared with her some of the happy memories that Tim and I had of John as a schoolboy and that I had of our five years together at Quarry Bank, long before John became world-famous. From our reminiscences, she could sense the camaraderie we shared as we grew up together. This helped her to feel closer to and to better understand the brother she hadn't known nearly as well as she would have liked, due to the significant age difference between them.

At the time we met, Julia was working on a book in which she wanted to set the record straight about her and John's mother, just as in writing this book, I am keen to set the record straight about John Lennon, the boy who became a legend. Tim and I were able to help Julia to fill in, from our perspective, some of the gaps in her knowledge of John's life that she was able to use in her very moving and readable book, *Imagine This*.

The author with John Lennon's half-sister, Julia Baird, and Tim Holmes at Tim's 65th birthday party at his home in Chester, September 2005.

The City of Liverpool was slow to recognise the enormous and continuing interest in The Beatles, and their origins, and to react so as to best capitalise on the huge commercial opportunities. But recognition belatedly came and Liverpool now provides Beatles nostalgia tours for visitors from all over the world, to visit places associated with the legendary group and its four famous members.

Not only is Mendips, the home of Aunt Mimi and Uncle George in which John spent most of his childhood, now a National Trust property (thanks to his widow, Yoko Ono, who bought and donated it) but Liverpool's Speke Airport is now named John Lennon Airport. John would have been gobsmacked by both of these things.

John Lennon:

There is no doubt that The Beatles helped to put Liverpool on the global map. People all over the world now identify Liverpool with The Beatles, more than with anything else. Perhaps this, added to the city's already long and rich musical and artistic heritage, helped it to become the European Capital of Culture in 2008. It seems entirely appropriate that John Lennon's sister, Julia, was made an official Ambassador for Liverpool.

The world is a richer place for having had John Lennon live in it for an all too short forty years, from 1940 to 1980. During his lifetime, and since his death, the music he made, alone and with Paul McCartney, George Harrison, Ringo Starr, Yoko Ono

Author at John Lennon's statue in A Coruña, Spain, 2012.

The Boy Who Became a Legend

and others, has given pleasure to countless millions of people throughout the world. John Lennon has touched us all. His music, and his message of peace and hope, will live forever.

Perhaps this book will give John's family and friends, and the world at large, an enhanced understanding of the complex, talented and sometimes troubled man who was John Lennon. In a world of increased spiritual enlightenment, John's spirit is alive and well. His presence is all around us.

John's friend, fellow Beatle and musical collaborator, Paul McCartney, at a concert in 2008 in Tel Aviv, Israel, sang John's emotive song "Give Peace A Chance". John would have liked that. Let's try to imagine, as he did, the world becoming a better place.

John Lennon: the boy who became a legend.
© *Eric Cash*

Author's Acknowledgements

This is a book that could have been written many years ago had I not been so absorbed in creating and managing a company that became, thanks to an outstanding team effort, Australia's market leading and most successful marine insurance organisation. That the book project commenced, following my retirement, and was finally ready for publication, is due in no small part to the support and encouragement I received from my family and friends. My sincere thanks go to all of them.

Experienced as I was in preparing business reports and conference papers, I had never written a book and had much to learn. Through The Writers' Workshop in England I found a very capable teacher in Martin Ouvry and I readily acknowledge his help.

I am grateful to my old school friends, Tim Holmes, Bob Hayes and Rod Davis for their memories of growing up with John Lennon in Liverpool.

For his enthusiasm for the book, reading the draft and contributing both ideas and photographs, I thank my good friend, Mark Naboshek, in Dallas, Texas. Thanks also to accomplished artist, Eric Cash, for his design work on the front and back cover and to Rod Davis for providing the photo image.

I owe a very big thank-you to my editor and Liverpool (or should I say Liddypool) identity, David Bedford, who enabled me, through the expertise of Rande Kessler, to have the book published.

Finally, my thanks to Randy Krone who, prompted by Mark Naboshek, approached David to try to help me get published. Just as there would have been no Beatles if Ivan Vaughan hadn't introduced Paul McCartney to John Lennon, this book about the formative years of John Lennon's life may never have been published if Randy hadn't brought me together with David.

Bibliography

JOHN LENNON–IN HIS OWN WRITE

John Lennon, published by Jonathan Cape Ltd., London, 1964

JOHN LENNON–IN MY LIFE

Pete Shotton and Nicholas Schaffner, published by Stein and Day Publishers, 1983

JOHN LENNON

Ray Coleman, published by Sidgwick & Jackson Ltd., London, 1984

THE BEATLES

Hunter Davies, published by Jonathan Cape Ltd, 1985

THE LIVES OF JOHN LENNON

Albert Goldman, published by William Morrow and Company, Inc., New York, 1988

THE BEATLES ANTHOLOGY

Published by Apple Corps Ltd., 2000.

THE QUARRYMEN

Hunter Davies, published by Omnibus Press (A Division of Music Sales Limited), 2001

The Boy Who Became a Legend

JOHN LENNON

Alan Clayson, published by Sanctuary Publishing Limited, 2003

JOHN LENNON - ALL I WANT IS THE TRUTH

Elizabeth Partridge, published by Penguin Group, 2005

IMAGINE THIS

Julia Baird, published by Hodder & Stoughton, 2007

JOHN LENNON – THE LIFE

Philip Norman, published by HarperCollins, 2008

LIDDYPOOL: BIRTHPLACE OF THE BEATLES

David Bedford, published by Dalton Watson Ltd. 2009

LENNON – THE MAN, THE MYTH, THE MUSIC

Tim Riley, published by Hyperion, New York, 2011

John Lennon:

Printed in Poland
by Amazon Fulfillment
Poland Sp. z o.o., Wrocław